THE CHRISTIAN WAY

A Wesleyan View of
Our Spiritual Journey

THE CHRISTIAN WAY

A Wesleyan View of Our Spiritual Journey

Maxie D. Dunnam

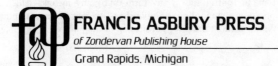
FRANCIS ASBURY PRESS
of Zondervan Publishing House

Grand Rapids, Michigan

THE CHRISTIAN WAY
Copyright © 1984, 1987 by Discipleship Resources
P.O. Box 840
Nashville, Tennessee 37202

FRANCIS ASBURY PRESS is an imprint of
Zondervan Publishing House
1415 Lake Drive, S.E.
Grand Rapids, Michigan 49506

Unless otherwise noted, all Scripture quotations are from the Revised
Standard Version of the Bible, copyright © 1946, 1952, 1971, 1973, by The
Division of Christian Education, National Council of the Churches of Christ
in the United States of America, and are used by permission.

All Scripture quotations marked "Amplified" are taken from *The Amplified
Bible,* copyright © 1965 by Zondervan Publishing House.

Scripture texts marked KJV are from the *King James Version.*

Cataloging in Publication Data
Dunnam, Maxie D.
        The Christian way.

        Based on: Our journey.
        Bibliography: p.
1. Spiritual life—Methodist authors. 2. Spirituality—Methodist church—
History of doctrines. 3. Methodist Church—Doctrines—History. I. Title.
BV4501.2.D7685 1987   230'.7   87-909
ISBN 0-310-20741-X

87 88 89 90 91 92 / CH / 9 8 7 6 5 4 3 2

Contents

TO
THE REVEREND DAVID H. McKEITHEN
who brought me into the Methodist fold and
guided my first stumbling steps in the ministry;

TO
The congregation of Christ United Methodist Church,
Memphis, Tennessee, who call forth the best that is in
me as preacher, allow me the joy of being their
pastor, and support me with their prayers and mutual
ministry—to whom the basic content of this book was
preached to launch our celebration of the Bicentennial
Year of Methodism in America;

AND TO
Methodist congregations I have served in McLain,
Beaumont, Leaf, Avant, Gautier, and Gulfport,
Mississippi; Atlanta, Georgia; San Clemente and
Anaheim, California. "I thank my God upon every
remembrance of you."

Introduction

I'm a Wesleyan by choice, though I have a great legacy of Christian experience from other traditions. My grandfather, Lewis Dunnam, was a Freewill Baptist preacher—the closest to a "circuit rider" we have in our family. He "walked" his circuit. I grew up in Southern and Missionary Baptist churches, but experienced throughout my childhood and early adolescence the brush arbor revivals of independent evangelists and the itinerant preachers who more often than not preached on the front porches of homes as folks stood around in the yards.

I was converted in a little Southern Baptist church in rural Mississippi and baptized at the hands of Brother Grissom in a rather cold creek in early September. My mother and father are active in that church today—my father, a deacon.

I knew only one Catholic before I went to college. He was a normal sort of fellow, but we thought it strange that he and his family would drive thirty miles each Sunday to get to a Catholic church for Mass. Interestingly, during the past fifteen years, Roman Catholic writers have been primary sources of spiritual nurture for me; and one of the most meaningful relationships I have is with the Ecumenical Institute of Spirituality—twenty-five persons, among whom are eight Roman Catholics, along with Quakers, Orthodox, Episcopalians, Lutherans, Presbyterians, and others.

I became a Methodist by choice about three years after my conversion. Doctrine had a lot to do with it—style also. But I wouldn't diminish the influence of a Methodist preacher, David McKeithen, a warm, loving human being who cared deeply for people, took time with a teen-age boy, and preached the gospel thoughtfully and with deep conviction. I began to feel the call to preach, and I felt that should I ever answer that call, I ought to be in the "right" church for me. I began to read and talk to people, and eventually I made the choice, surprising David and his congregation when I walked down the aisle on a Sunday morning to offer myself as a member. Then a year later, I offered myself to that same congregation as a candidate for ministry.

So, I'm a Wesleyan by choice, and it thrilled me when I was invited to write this book.

As I began this work, a cartoon came to my attention. It pictured a pastor in a very large pulpit. His head was withdrawn deep into his shoulders as if he were trying to escape something. His mouth was turned downward; his eyes looked blank. He was truly forlorn; he was a pitiful sight. There was a layman beside the pulpit obviously trying to help him, but what he was doing was unusual. On a nearby stool was a large battery, and the clips of a jumper cable had been attached to the terminals. The layman had a clip in each hand, and he was reaching toward the pastor. The top of the pastor's head had been swung open, and the layman was reaching in with the jumper cable.

10

In the foreground of the cartoon was the front row of the congregation. A smiling woman was leaning over to speak to some folks who were obviously visitors. She said very matter-of-factly, "Sometimes the pastor needs a little help to get started."

Funny as it is, it's true. It's hard to get started—not just on a sermon but on a book like this. How do you begin to talk about the Christian way of life as the Wesleys and early Methodists saw it? In a volume this size, decisions of emphasis have to be made, and some things we hold firmly have to be left out. This is tough, but essential.

I'm not going to deal specifically with that which we hold in common with all orthodox Christians, such as our belief in the Trinity, in God, in Jesus Christ, in the Holy Spirit, in the Bible, in the Resurrection, and so on. Rather, I want to deal with the way of salvation as understood and experienced in the Wesleyan movement. That doesn't mean that what I say about a particular theme will be unique to Wesleyanism; it simply means that I'm going to put together in these chapters that which, as I understand it, is the heartbeat, the distinct content, and to some degree the style of who we are as Wesleyans—particularly as viewed by John Wesley.

The reason it's so hard for me to get started is that I am basically an impatient person. I have problems pacing myself; therefore, my temptation is to want to say it all. I don't want to leave out anything. Also, I have this almost neurotic passion to speak freshly and, at the same time, clearly. So I find myself wrestling with the dilemma of expressing a 2,000-year-old gospel, and our 250-year-old Wesleyan expression of that gospel, in a fresh way. I probably ought simply to relax and concentrate on clarity.

Now that I have made that confession, I feel better. Whether it helps you, the reader, or not is another question.

The central theme of each chapter will be rooted in a particular passage of Scripture. I have done this deliberately to underscore Wesley's claim that he was a person of "one Book," and to call us Wesleyans back to the primary source of our life as individuals and in the church. A recovery of an emphasis upon Scripture is one of the crucial needs in Wesleyanism.

I have also deliberately quoted Wesley frequently. We need to read Wesley more if we are going to be faithful to our heritage; but more, we need to read him in order to capture the same Spirit that controlled his life and brought revival to England and America. Yet, I have also sought to put the message in our contemporary setting and experiential need.

It is my prayer that this effort will make a contribution to the renewal of our church as we discover or rediscover the unique place we have in God's family. We need to recover that uniqueness, not to set us apart from others, but to help us be the people God wants us to be. God would be pleased, I think, if we would take up again the mission that was declared when the Wesleyan movement first put its roots down in this new land: "To reform a continent and spread scriptural holiness across the land." Any reflection on the Wesleyan heritage will be for naught unless it gives us a new vision and thrusts us into the future as Spirit-filled and Spirit-led people.

MAXIE D. DUNNAM

1
The Keystone: Salvation by Faith

And you he made alive, when you were dead through the trespasses and sins in which you once walked. . . . But God, who is rich in mercy, out of the great love with which he loved us, even when we were dead through our trespasses, made us alive together with Christ (by grace you have been saved), and raised us up with him, and made us sit with him in the heavenly places in Christ Jesus, that in the coming ages he might show the immeasurable riches of his grace in kindness toward us in Christ Jesus. For by grace you have been saved through faith; and this is not your own doing, it is the gift of God—not because of works, lest any man should boast. For we are his workmanship, created in Christ Jesus for good works, which God prepared beforehand, that we should walk in them (Eph. 2:1–2, 4–10).

If you were asked, What is the goal of your life? how would you respond? To be happy? To have a healthy, happy family? To be a success in business? To be wealthy? To serve other people and make others happy? To find the right marriage mate? To be fulfilled in your profession? Listen to the founder of Wesleyanism, John Wesley:

To candid, reasonable men, I'm not afraid to lay open what have been the inmost thoughts of my heart. I have thought, I'm a creature of a day, passing through life as

THE CHRISTIAN WAY

an arrow through the air. I am a spirit come from God, and returning to God: Just hovering over the great gulf; til a few moments hence, I am no more seen; I drop into an unchangeable eternity. I want to know one thing—the way to heaven; how to land safe on that happy shore. God Himself has condescended to teach the way; for this very end He came from heaven. He hath written it down in a book. O give me that book! At any price, give me the Book of God![1]

This word expressed the fire burning in Wesley's soul: "I want to know one thing—the way to heaven; how to land safe on that happy shore." This desire of Wesley was like that passionate expression of Paul to the Philippians:

Not that I have already obtained this or am already perfect; but I press on to make it my own, because Christ Jesus has made me his own. Brethren, I do not consider that I have made it my own; but one thing I do, forgetting what lies behind and straining forward to what lies ahead, I press on toward the goal for the prize of the upward call of God in Christ Jesus (Phil. 3:12–14).

The goal of Wesley's life was his own salvation. History verifies that once he was certain of that—his own salvation— the passion became other-directed, and he started one of the great revivals of history as he sought to share the salvation message with others. Over and over in his *Journal,* he recorded his preaching activity in his simple sentence: "I offered them Christ."

John Wesley published four volumes of sermons—in 1746, 1748, 1750, and 1760. In 1763, he prepared a model deed for his preaching houses that set forth his intentions after his death. In that deed, it was provided that persons appointed by the conference should "have and enjoy the premises" only on condition "that the said persons preach no other doctrine than is contained in Mr. Wesley's Notes upon the New Testament and four volumes of sermons."[2]

"Salvation by Faith" was the first of Wesley's standard

sermons. So this is where we begin, the keystone of his understanding of Christian doctrine—"salvation by faith."

Paul developed this theme systematically in his Letter to the Romans. His Galatian letter was an expression of the same truth primarily from his heart, not his head. Our Scripture from Ephesians is a spontaneous outpouring of this conviction about salvation by faith in the midst of a commentary on the nature and mission of the church.

Since Paul, volumes have been written on this theme of salvation by faith; and I boldly propose to capture the essence of it (at least enough for us to go on) in this chapter by asking, in the style of Mr. Wesley's sermon on this theme, three questions:

1. Who needs it?
2. What is it we need?
3. How do we get it?

WHO NEEDS SALVATION?

First, who needs it? The answer is clear, simple, and encompassing: We all need it.

Paul stated our predicament: "And you he made alive, when you were dead through the trespasses and sins in which you once walked, following the course of this world, following the prince of the power of the air, the spirit that is now at work in the sons of disobedience" (Eph. 2:1–2).

In Romans 3, Paul dealt specifically with the universality of sin, quoting passages from five psalms and one verse from Isaiah. Consider his terrible word:

> None is righteous, no, not one;
> no one understands, no one seeks for God.
> All have turned aside, together they have gone
> wrong;
> no one does good, not even one.
> Their throat is an open grave,
> they use their tongues to deceive.
> The venom of asps is under their lips.

15

Their mouth is full of curses and bitterness.
Their feet are swift to shed blood,
   in their paths are ruin and misery,
   and the way of peace they do not know.
There is no fear of God before their eyes
                    (Rom. 3:10–18).

Paul began this catalog of our common predicament by contending that we are all under sin. Think about that for a moment.

Charles Gatemouth Brown is one of America's foremost composers and singers of "blues" music. He is the recipient of a Grammy and, in 1983, the winner of the W. T. Handy Blues Award. In an interview on ABC News, he said, "Anyone who has brains gets the blues."

That's universal, isn't it? Paul and John Wesley would express the same universal compass of sin: "Anyone who is human is a sinner."

Paul contended that all people, "both Jews and Greeks, are under the power of sin" (Rom. 3:9). The Greek phrase that he used for this state of being under sin when we are without Christ was *hupo hamartian,* which means "in the power of sin" or "under the authority of sin." You get the scope of it by seeing the way Paul used the word *hupo* in other places. He described the relationship of a schoolboy to his teacher as being "under a schoolmaster" (Gal. 3:25 KJV). In 1 Timothy 6:1, he said slaves were "under the yoke." In both instances, to be "under" (*hupo*) means to be "dominated by" or "under the authority of."

That's the predicament of all of us with regard to sin. Paul said, "For there is no distinction; since all have sinned and fall short of the glory of God" (Rom. 3:22–23).

Do you have problems believing that? Is Paul's description too terrible? In another chapter, we will deal with the whole issue of "original sin." For now, let's not debate the universality of sin, but seek to see where we are in the picture. Without dealing with such glaring sins as committing adultery, killing, and stealing, answer these questions:

16

— Do you sometimes think more highly of yourself than you ought to think?
— Is there any person of whom you are jealous?
— Do you occasionally look at a person of the opposite sex and feel lust in your heart?
— Do you sometimes hate people of other races or nations?
— Do you get anxious about the future because you feel you don't have enough financial security?
— Do you judge others by what they have? By their station in life? Whether they are cultured or not? Their level of educational achievement?

Those questions sound innocent, don't they? And most of us would answer yes to a number of them. Do you know what that means? It means that we are among those Paul was describing: "All have sinned and fall short of the glory of God."

Who needs it? Who needs salvation? We all do!

WHAT SALVATION DO WE NEED?

The second question is, What is it we need? We need salvation. What is the nature of this salvation?

Let's take our cue directly from Scripture. Paul described the result of sin in our lives: "You were dead through the trespasses and sins." You were not in control of your life—you followed "the course of this world" like a puppet controlled by Satan. This meant that you lived in the passions of your flesh, "following the desires of body and mind."

But then something happened. God "made us alive together with Christ." It's a dramatic distinction. Sin equals death—we were dead; salvation equals life—God made us live. This is an echo of Paul's whole life. He knew himself to be a great sinner, but he knew Christ to be a great Savior. He never understated or underplayed sin in our lives; nor did he understate or underplay the redeeming power of Jesus Christ. So it was with John Wesley.

17

The salvation we need and the salvation Christ affords is the salvation from sin. Be clear about this. It is a *present* salvation. Paul did not say to the Ephesians, "You *will be* saved." He said, "You *have been* saved." The work is accomplished now. Let us see how this happens at the point of three great needs:

1. *We are saved from the guilt of all past sins.* Paul put it graphically in Colossians 2:13–14. We have been forgiven all our sins; "the bond which stood against us with its legal demands" has been set aside, canceled, *nailed to the cross.*

What a descriptive metaphor! Nothing can be more dramatic or powerful—to know that when Jesus was nailed to the cross, *our sins,* my sins, your sins, and the guilt therefrom were nailed to the cross. I see this demonstrated over and over again.

A fifty-year-old woman (let's call her Mary) was devastated with guilt over estrangement from and hatred of her father. Mary's mother had died of cancer. During the last months of her life, her husband had courted another woman; he married her almost immediately after the death of his wife. Mary's hatred for her father and his new wife was venomous. She refused to have anything to do with them. She finally came to see that hatred was destroying her. Then she became plagued with guilt over fifteen years of estrangement from her father. Her guilt paralyzed her. She wanted reconciliation, but she could not take the initiative in the relationship. The father had given up long ago.

At the close of a worship service in which the theme of forgiveness—salvation from all past sin and guilt—had been proclaimed, Mary and I shared and prayed together for about an hour. Mary believed, accepted the forgiveness of grace, and claimed salvation for herself. That very night she wrote to her father and began the process of reconciliation and the reclaiming and rebuilding of a daughter-father love and relationship.

2. We are saved from the guilt of all past sins, and *we are also saved from fear.* Fear is the twin of guilt and burns

18

almost as ravagingly as guilt itself in many of our lives—fear of God's judgment, of eternal punishment, of God's wrath.

But the salvation Christ affords takes away our fear. We now know not the wrath of God, but God's extravagant love. We "have not received the spirit of bondage again to fear; but . . . have received the Spirit of adoption, whereby we cry, Abba, Father. The Spirit itself beareth witness with our spirit, that we are the children of God" (Rom. 8:15–16 KJV).

John Wesley would remind us that we are also saved from the fear, though not from the possibility, of falling away from the grace of God and coming short of God's great and precious promises. That is a unique understanding of Wesleyanism. We will return to it later. We are saved from the fear, though not from the possibility, of falling away from the grace of God. We are "sealed with the promised Holy Spirit, which is the guarantee of our inheritance" (Eph. 1:13–14).

We have peace with God through our Lord Jesus Christ. We rejoice in the hope of the glory of God, and the love of God is shed abroad in our hearts, through the Holy Spirit, who is given to us.

And hereby we are persuaded, though perhaps not at all times, nor with the same fullness of persuasion, that neither death nor life, nor things present nor things to come, nor height, nor depth, nor any creature shall be able to separate us from the love of God, which is in Christ Jesus our Lord (see Rom. 8:38–39).

We are saved from fear.

3. The last word about the nature of our salvation is that *we are saved from the power of sin*. We will discuss this more fully in chapter 4, but it must be noted now. Paul was very clear about the fact that unredeemed persons live under the power of sin. He was also triumphantly clear about the fact that Christ frees us from the power of sin. "He has delivered us from the dominion of darkness and transferred us to the kingdom of his beloved Son" (Col. 1:13). This was Wesley's deep conviction. Charles Wesley sang joyfully about this fact:

> Long my imprisoned spirit lay,
> Fast bound in sin and nature's night,
> Thine eye diffused a quickening ray;
> I woke, the dungeon flamed with light;
> My chains fell off, my heart was free,
> I rose, went forth, and followed Thee.[3]

So what is it we need? Salvation that is a present reality—salvation from sin, from the guilt and fear that result from sin, and from the power of sin over us.

HOW DO WE RECEIVE SALVATION?

The final question is, How do we get it? And the answer is, We don't get it; *it is given.*

Isn't it strange that we have as many problems with this fact as any other? One of the crucial debates of Christian doctrine has swirled around this issue. How are we to be saved? Two theories have been set forth as to how we are reconciled to God: One is by *works,* the other by *faith.* We underscore again Paul's words from Ephesians 2:8–9. "For by grace you have been saved through faith; and this is not your own doing, it is the gift of God—not because of works, lest any man should boast." How do we get it? We don't; it is given. Salvation is by faith and faith alone.

In Romans 3:23–25, Paul stated the truth about salvation as a gift in this fashion: "Since all have sinned and fall short of the glory of God, they are justified by his grace as a gift, through the redemption which is in Christ Jesus, whom God put forward as an expiation by his blood, to be received by faith." The Greek word for expiation "refers to the sacrifices offered to pagan deities, as a means of appeasing their displeasure and averting their anger."[4] Some theologians transferred this concept to the New Testament and saw Christ's sacrifice as a means of placating an angry God. Others have objected to this interpretation on the grounds that it demeans God's nature, that it reduces God to the level of a petty pagan deity. A different view emphasizes the fact that this word is used in the Greek translation of the Old Testament to translate the phrase *Mercy Seat.* In Hebrew ritual, the high-priest appeared before the Ark of the Covenant, which contained the stone tablets of the Law. The priest sprinkled blood from a sacrifice on the golden lid of the Ark which was called the Mercy Seat. The symbolism richly portrayed the fact that a broken law stood between God and the people, but through the shedding of blood, the place of judgment and estrangement became the place of mercy and reconciliation. Christ's death is therefore seen as the means whereby God's demand for justice against a sinful race is fully met, thereby freeing God to be merciful to those who formally merited only judgment.[5]

Here is a picture from the human scene that will help us understand this magnificent truth: One of the most beautiful and moving love stories that I have ever heard is that of Thomas Moore, the nineteenth-century Irish poet. Shortly after his marriage, he was called away on business. It was some time before he returned home, and when he did, he found waiting for him at the front door of the house not his beautiful bride, but the family doctor.

"Your wife is upstairs," said the doctor, "but she's asked that you do not come up." Then Thomas Moore learned the terrible truth: His wife had contracted smallpox. The disease had left her once flawless skin pocked and scarred. She had taken one look at her reflection in the mirror and had commanded that the shutters be drawn and that her husband never see her again.

Moore would not listen. He ran upstairs and opened the door to his wife's room. It was black as night inside. Not a sound came from the darkness. Groping along the wall, Moore grasped for the gas jets.

A startled cry came from the black corner of the room. "No! Don't light the lamps!"

Moore hesitated, swayed by the pleading in the voice. "Go!" she begged. "Please go! This is the greatest gift I can give you now."

Moore did go. He went down to his study where he sat up most of the night, prayerfully writing—not a poem this time, but a song. He had never written a song before, but it seemed more in keeping with his mood than a poem. He not only wrote the words, he wrote the music too. The next morning as soon as the sun was up, he returned to his wife's room. He felt his way to a chair and sat down. "Are you awake?" he asked.

"I am," came a voice from the far side of the room. "But you must not ask to see me. You must not press me, Thomas."

"I will sing to you, then," he answered. And so for the first time, Thomas Moore sang to his wife the song that still lives today:

> Believe me, if all those endearing young charms,
>   which I gaze on so fondly today,
> Were to change by tomorrow and flee from
>   my arms,
>   like fairy gifts fading away,
> Thou wouldst still be adored, as this moment
>   thou art . . .

He heard a movement from the dark corner where his wife lay in her loneliness, waiting. He continued:

> Let thy loveliness fade as it will,
> and round the dear ruin each wish of my heart
> Would entwine itself verdantly still.

The song ended. As his voice trailed off the last note, Moore heard his bride arise. She crossed the room to the window, reached up, and slowly drew open the shutters. That is the power of love. And that is only a hint of the love of Christ for us.

We don't deserve that love. We can't earn it. It is given. Ravaged by the guilt and fear that result from this dreadful disease, pocked and scarred as we are by sin, we hear the love song of God: "For God sent the Son into the world, not to condemn the world, but that the world might be saved through him" (John 3:17). We see that music translated into the sacrificial action of Christ on the cross. To this place of extravagant love and mercy we come, believing that Christ died for us, and miraculously the shutters are opened upon our dark world of sin, guilt, and fear. Our lives are flooded with the light of God's salvation, and He makes us "alive together with Christ," forever freed from the bondage of sin.

That is the keystone of Wesley's doctrine—salvation by faith—and it is all rooted in God's grace, which is the theme of our next chapter.

2
Amazing Grace

For God so loved the world that he gave his only Son, that whoever believes in him should not perish but have eternal life. For God sent the Son into the world, not to condemn the world, but that the world might be saved through him. He who believes in him is not condemned; he who does not believe is condemned already, because he has not believed in the name of the only Son of God. And this is the judgment, that the light has come into the world, and men loved darkness rather than light, because their deeds were evil (John 3:16-19).

But now the righteousness of God has been manifested apart from law, although the law and the prophets bear witness to it, the righteousness of God through faith in Jesus Christ for all who believe. For there is no distinction; since all have sinned and fall short of the glory of God, they are justified by his grace as a gift, through the redemption which is in Christ Jesus, whom God put forward as an expiation by his blood, to be received by faith. This was to show God's righteousness, because in his divine forbearance he had passed over former sins; it was to prove at the present time that he himself is righteous and that he justifies him who has faith in Jesus (Rom. 3:21-26).

The proclamation of the Christian gospel is not restricted to pulpits and Sunday school classrooms. The January 9, 1984, issue of *Time* magazine carried on its cover a full-color picture of Pope John Paul II and his would-be killer Mehmet Ali Agca. The pope is shaking Ali Agca's hand, and his other hand is around Agca's shoulder. A one-inch type insert spans the picture, drawing the two men even closer together. The bold question of the print is, WHY FORGIVE?

The cover story was excellent, proclaiming with evangelical zeal that a pardon from the pontiff was a lesson in forgiveness in a troubled world.

Most readers of the magazine had probably forgotten the story of the attempted assassination that had taken place in Rome's St. Peter's Square in May 1981. Violence is so common. Spectacles of revenge and terror occur so regularly that we pass them off almost as soon as they happen.

But when it happened, it shocked the world as the picture was captured on TV and in newspapers. Pope John Paul II, in white robes, was capsized backward on his seat, stricken, in a posture reminiscent of the *Pietà*. There was a dramatic burst of emotion and shock in the scene as the security men sprang alive and the Pontiff's white "popemobile" lurched through the crowd. The pope had been shot.

Ordinarily, a spasm of savagery such as that simply passes and recedes in time—an ugly, vague memory if recalled at all. But in an extraordinary moment of grace, the memory of that violence in St. Peter's Square was transformed. *Time* magazine told the story:

> In a bare white-walled cell in Rome's Rebibbia Prison, John Paul tenderly held the hand that had held the gun that was meant to kill him. For twenty-one minutes the Pope sat with his would-be assassin Mehmet Ali Agca. The two talked softly. Once or twice, Ali Agca laughed. The Pope forgave him for the shooting. At the end of the meeting, Agca either kissed the Pope's ring or pressed the Pope's hand to his forehead in a Moslem gesture of relief.

25

It was a startling drama of forgiveness and reconciliation.[1]

It was a moving picture of grace that was the primary theme of John Wesley, Philip William Otterbein, and Jacob Albright. It is a core belief for the Wesleyan Christian.

Time magazine is not unaware of the power of pictures and the dramatic use of imagery. The magnificent article was punctuated with pictures, photographic vignettes, that set the question "Why forgive?" deep in the stark reality of violence that is the signature of a world gone mad. There was the picture of the pope when he was shot, held from collapsing by another person. There was a picture of Beirut in the chaotic aftermath of a terrorist car bomb explosion; the eyes of the closest man in the picture portray a haunting terror that comes either from paralyzing fear or from raging anger. There was also a picture of a shabby, bare room of the Sabra Refugee Camp in Lebanon; stretched out on the cold, dirty floor of that room was the lifeless body of a pregnant Palestinian woman.

There were other pictures—but one was missing. The drama of grace and forgiveness would have been complete with a picture of Calvary—three crosses against a dark, stormy sky, with Jesus hanging on the center one, struggling to speak that final word of grace, "Father, forgive them."

Grace—amazing grace—is the heart of the Christian gospel. John captured it in John 3:16. And Paul argued it so convincingly in Romans 3:23–25.

John Wesley did us a great service and provided us with a distinctive emphasis by talking about grace impinging upon us and working in three specific ways: (1) prevenient grace, (2) justifying grace, and (3) sanctifying grace. Prevenient grace is the grace of God going before us, pulling us, wooing us, seeking to open our minds and hearts, and eventually giving us faith. Justifying grace is the forgiving love of God, freely given to us, reconciling us, putting us right with God, making Christ, who knew no sin, to be sin on our behalf. Sanctifying grace is the work and Spirit of Christ within us, restoring the broken image, completing the salvation that was begun in justification, and bringing us to complete newness of life and perfection in love.

We will discuss sanctifying grace in chapter 4. Here we will look at prevenient grace and justifying grace.

PREVENIENT GRACE

I have a picture in my office—a painting by my wife Jerry. You have to study many paintings to get their meaning, and sometimes the meaning you get is not what the artist intended. I heard of a person who went into a museum of modern art. Looking around at what to him was a horrid onslaught of color and distorted design, he commented, "There is less here than meets the eye."

My wife doesn't paint that way, but this piece is an impressionistic design of color and movement, dominantly blue, from deep shades to translucent light. The person in this painting, engulfed in the flow of color, is not obvious at first glance. As you study the painting, you can see that the person stands in the swirl of color and movement surrounded by light and life that come from somewhere beyond; yet you know that the light and movement energize and give the person life.

Jerry called her painting "Grace" because it is the expression of her experience of God's love as proclaimed in the hymn, "I Sought the Lord." At a particular time of struggle in her life, the hymn ministered to her, and her painting flowed from that experience.

27

I sought the Lord, and afterward I knew
  He moved my soul to seek him, seeking me;
It was not I that found, O Savior true;
  No, I was found of thee.

Thou didst reach forth thy hand and mine enfold;
  I walked and sank not on the storm-vexed sea;
'Twas not so much that I on thee took hold
  As thou, dear Lord, on me.[2]

That's the nature of prevenient grace. The Lord seeks us before we begin to seek. Wesley sounded this note strongly in opposition to a doctrine of predestination. Whether the rigid, double predestination idea—that some are damned to hell while others are elected for heaven, or another variation on that theme—the doctrine of predestination has as its center an understanding of grace as limited. For Wesley—and this is another particularly Wesleyan emphasis—grace is universal. It is "free in all, and free for all." Bishop William R. Cannon makes the case:

> To be sure, it is free to all in the sense that it is given without price, that it does not demand anything of us before it is bestowed, and that it flows from the free mercy of God. But note the change. Grace is free *for all*. It is not free only for those whom God has ordained to life, but it is like the air we breathe, or the wind that blows in our faces; it is for everyone who dwells upon the face of the earth.[3]

Now that doesn't mean that all persons receive this grace or deliberately appropriate it or respond to it for their salvation. They don't. That is the reason we began with the emphasis on faith in the first chapter. For salvation, we must respond in faith to God's grace. But let's continue looking specifically at the nature of God's amazing grace.

Prevenient grace (or "preventing grace") is *the grace that comes before*. What does that mean? It means that before any conscious personal experience of divine grace, grace is there, working in our lives. The first move is God's, not ours. This is the witness of the Scripture. As clear as anything else in the Bible is the fact that God seeks us. God is, as Francis Thompson would say, "the hound of heaven" who relentlessly pursues us. That's the story over and over again in the Bible—a searching God who takes the initiative in human life.

It all began with Adam and Eve in the garden. When they had sinned, they experienced guilt. They did not want to see God, nor did they want God to see them, so they hid. But

God came looking for them, calling them by name, "Adam, Eve, where are you?"

Moses hid from God in Midian. He didn't want God to find him because he knew what God was going to ask him to do.

The story goes on: Elijah hid in a cave. Peter tried to hide his Galilean accent from those around the fire in the courtyard outside the place where Jesus was on trial.

That is the story: people hiding, God seeking. Jesus underscored it with the three parables Luke put together for "the gospel in the Gospel"—the parables of the lost coin, the lost sheep, and the lost son. That's the point of view of the Bible, what the Scripture is all about—the story of God's searching for us. Most of us thought it was the other way around, didn't we? We thought the Bible was the story about people who were looking for God. That really isn't so. It's the story of God's seeking us.

In his underscoring of prevenient grace, Wesley echoed Peter's word that God is "not wishing that any should perish, but that all should reach repentance" (2 Pet. 3:9).

Prevenient grace is not only the grace that comes before, meaning that God takes the first step in our redemption; it is a *leading grace*. It is the activity of the Spirit in our lives, moving us to a place of repentance and reconciliation.

Wesley noted three ways in which prevenient grace leads us: (1) It creates in us our first sensitivity to God's call, to God's seeking us, to God's will. (2) It produces an awareness and conviction that we have violated God's will and are not responsive to the divine call. This conviction may be slight and transient, but it is real and is a part of God's prevenient grace working in us. (3) Prevenient grace stimulates our first wish to please God.

These three workings of prevenient grace in our lives, according to Wesley, lead us to repentance, which is a necessary step to salvation. It is important to underscore what we noted earlier. God's grace is universal, but prevenient grace is not sufficient for salvation. Persons may suppress or ignore this grace. If so, Scripture warns that we may experience hardness of heart, so that these stirrings of the Spirit within will go unheeded. (We will look at this again when we discuss free will and predestination in the next chapter.)

Review a bit. Wesley said grace is "free in all, and free for all." No one is excluded from the work of prevenient grace. Grace is *for* all, a gift from God. But we must respond to prevenient grace if we are to experience its justifying power.

JUSTIFYING GRACE

The resounding word of the New Testament is that we are justified by grace. That's good news!

Have you heard the story of the man who came home one night feeling very sorry for himself? Nothing had gone right at the office. It was one of those days when there seemed to be one hassle after another. When he arrived home, he could tell by the look on his wife's face that she had probably had the same kind of day. Before she could say anything, he said, "I don't know what your day has been like, and I don't know what you're getting ready to tell me, but if it's bad news, please keep it to yourself. I've had all the bad news I can stand for one day."

She looked at him with some uncertainty and then said, "Well, maybe it is good news. You know we have six wonderful children." He said, "That's right." Then she said, "You'll be happy to know that five of them did not break an arm today."

Good news or bad news is sometimes a matter of perspective. The bad news of our life is that we have all sinned and fallen short of the glory of God. The good news is that God is gracious, and although we deserve condemnation, we are justified. God delivers us. We are saved by grace.

Justification is the common word used to describe what God does freely for us through grace. It is a metaphor

primarily from the law courts. Keep in mind these questions:
How can we as sinners get into a right relationship with God?
How are we able to feel at peace, at ease, at home with God?
How can we escape the feeling of fear in the presence of
God—the sense of estrangement, of judgment? That's the
problem. Judaism answered the questions this way: A person
can attain a right relationship with God by keeping the law. By
fulfilling all the works of the law, a person will be right with
God. But condemnation is implicit in this, for no one can live
in perfect obedience, keeping every law. Salvation is not a
way of works; it is a way of faith.

Justification is based on the imagery of being on trial
before God. *Dikaioun* is the Greek word translated "to
justify." William Barclay provides helpful insight into this
word.[4] He notes that all Greek verbs that end in *-oun* mean
not to "make" someone something, but "to treat, to reckon,
or to account" someone as something. The point about God's
relationship to us is this: When we appear before God, we are
anything but innocent; we are utterly guilty. And yet God
treats us, reckons us, accounts us as if we were innocent. That
is what justification means.

When Paul said that "God justifies the ungodly," he
meant that God, in incredible mercy, treats us as if we were
godly people. This is what shocked the Jews. To treat a bad
man as if he were a good man was the sign of a wicked judge.
"He who justifies the wicked and he who condemns the
righteous are both alike an abomination to the LORD" (Prov.
17:15). "I will not justify the wicked" (Exod. 23:7 KJV). But
Paul said that is precisely what God does.

Though justification is a metaphor of the law court, we
cannot understand the grace of God's justifying us unless we
see sin as a crime against love, not as a crime against law. To
be sure, in sin we break God's law; but more important, we
break God's heart. We may atone for a broken law, but how
do we atone for a broken heart?

We have a painting in our bedroom that would not be
considered great art, but it has profound meaning for us. It

31

was painted by a friend who was a member of one of our former congregations. The painting is of a little black girl with haunting eyes that reflect a mixture of sadness and hope. Mary Jo started painting as therapy for the deep sorrow of her life, and this painting was one of her first.

One afternoon, she and her three daughters were at the shopping center that was within walking distance of their home. She was carrying the baby, and the other two little blonde, blue-eyed girls were walking along where they should have been—ahead of her on the sidewalk. It happened without warning. An elderly man coming out of a parking place bumped another car, panicked, and hit the gas pedal instead of the brake. The car jumped the curb, crashed into one of the little girls, and threw her through the guardrail along the sidewalk and into a ravine below. She was dead—before her mother's eyes.

I don't know what happened to the driver. Drivers whose carelessness or recklessness takes lives are usually arrested, tried, found guilty, and fined; sometimes they are imprisoned; sometimes their driving privileges are taken away. But after such persons have paid their fines or served their sentences, the law has no further claim upon them. As far as the law is concerned, justice has been served. The matter is over.

But that doesn't touch the issue of the parents' hearts or the heart of the driver himself. The driver of the car that snuffed out the life of our little friend could never make things up to her parents, never put things right, by serving a sentence or paying a fine. Love—parent-love—had ended in heart-break for all, and only the forgiveness of the little girl's parents could restore the relationship between them and the driver.

That is the way it is in our relationship with God. We may have broken God's laws, but the terrible tragedy is that we've broken God's heart. Only an act of the free forgiveness of God's grace can bring us back into relationship with Him. And that's what the Cross is all about—*amazing grace, justifying us.*

I think about that amazing grace when I look at Mary Jo's painting. She forgave the man who killed her child and worked out her grief by painting the likeness of little children from all over the world. The little black girl in our bedroom is one of those children. As I look into her sad but hopeful eyes, I am reminded that God is saddened by our sinfulness, but hopeful—always hopeful—that none of us will perish but that all of us will come to repentance.

There is so much at the heart of grace, which we Wesleyans believe to be the core of the gospel and Christian experience, that we need to look longer at this justifying aspect of grace. We do so by focusing again on Paul's word: "Since all have sinned and fall short of the glory of God, they are justified by his grace as a gift, through the redemption which is in Christ Jesus, whom God put forward as an expiation by his blood, to be received by faith" (Rom. 3:23–25).

Three metaphors in this passage help us understand justifying grace. The first is *justification*, the metaphor from the law courts that we have already discussed. Before God's court, we are utterly guilty. Yet, in amazing mercy, God *trusts* us, *reckons* us, *accounts* us as innocent. When we believe that God loves us and that Christ died for us, and when we trust God's loving activity in Jesus Christ for our salvation, we are justified.

That leads to the second metaphor, that of *sacrifice*. Paul said that God put forward Jesus Christ as an expiation (or propitiation) for our sin. The Greek word translated as "propitiation" or "expiation" has to do with sacrifice. The offering of sacrifices was prominent in the Jewish religion of the Old Testament, but was also present in most ancient religions. The purpose of these sacrifices was to avert the wrath of God. The pattern in the Old Testament was the offering of animal sacrifices. But even in the Old Testament, there are the stirrings that such sacrifices were not adequate. David stated it clearly out of the anguish of his own sin and guilt: "For thou hast no delight in sacrifice; were I to give a

33

burnt offering, thou wouldst not be pleased. The sacrifice acceptable to God is a broken spirit; a broken and contrite heart, O God, thou wilt not despise" (Ps. 51:16–17). Likewise, Micah made the case: "With what shall I come before the LORD, and bow myself before God on high? Shall I come before him with burnt offerings, with calves a year old? Will the LORD be pleased with thousands of rams, with ten thousands of rivers of oil? Shall I give my first-born for my transgression, the fruit of my body for the sin of my soul?" (Mic. 6:6–7).

Paul concluded that only one sacrifice was sufficient— the sacrifice Jesus made on the cross. That sacrifice alone can atone and open the door to God that no other effort or action can accomplish.

The third metaphor is taken from *slavery*. Paul spoke of the redemption, or deliverance, which is in Christ Jesus. The Greek word is *apolutrōsis* and means "a ransoming, a redeeming, a liberating." It means that we are in the power, the grip, the dominion of sin, and Christ alone can free us.

None of these metaphors alone is adequate. All of them together still do not probe the depth of the mystery. It is the mystery of what God does for us in Jesus Christ that we cannot do for ourselves. It is justifying us when we are utterly guilty, providing a sacrifice when we have nothing to offer, setting us free when we are powerless to break the strong tentacles of sin. Wesley provided a good summary of it:

> This then is the salvation which is through faith, even in the present world: a salvation from sin, and the consequences of sin, both often expressed in the word *justification*; which, taken in the largest sense, implies a deliverance from guilt and punishment, by the atonement of Christ actually applied to the soul of the sinner now believing on Him, and a deliverance from the (whole body) of sin, through Christ *formed in his heart*. So that he who is thus justified, or saved by faith, is indeed *born again*. He is *born again of the Spirit* into a new life, which "is hid with Christ in God." (He is a new creature:

34

old things are passed away: all things in him are become new.) And as a newborn babe, he gladly receives the . . . "*sincere* milk of the word, and grows thereby"; going on in the might of the Lord his God, from faith to faith, from grace to grace, until at length, he comes unto "a perfect man, unto the measure of the stature of the fullness of Christ."[5]

In the next chapter we will look specifically at the power of sin in our lives, the sin from which we are freed. Then in chapter 4 we will return to Wesley's theme song, *grace,* as we consider sanctifying grace, or Christian perfection.

35

3
Sin: There's Nothing Original About It!

Did that which is good, then, bring death to me? By no means! It was sin, working death in me through what is good, in order that sin might be shown to be sin, and through the commandment might become sinful beyond measure. We know that the law is spiritual; but I am carnal, sold under sin. I do not understand my own actions. For I do not do what I want, but I do the very thing I hate. Now if I do what I do not want, I agree that the law is good. So then it is no longer I that do it, but sin which dwells within me. For I know that nothing good dwells within me, that is, in my flesh. I can will what is right, but I cannot do it. For I do not do the good I want, but the evil I do not want is what I do. Now if I do what I do not want, it is no longer I that do it, but sin which dwells within me. So I find it to be a law that when I want to do right, evil lies close at hand. For I delight in the law of God, in my inmost self, but I see in my members another law at war with the law of my mind and making me captive to the law of sin which dwells in my members. Wretched man that I am! Who will deliver me from this body of death? Thanks be to God through Jesus Christ our Lord! So then, I of myself serve the law of God with my mind, but with my flesh I serve the law of sin. There is therefore now no condemnation for those who are in Christ Jesus. For the law of the Spirit of life in Christ Jesus has set me free from the law of sin and death (Rom. 7:13–8:2).

Somewhere along the way I heard of a little Christian college in Arkansas that advertised in its bulletin that it was sixteen miles from any known sin.

I grew up in the backwoods of Mississippi, and I know that Arkansas and Mississippi are a lot alike. But nowhere in my backwoods Mississippi could you get six miles, much less sixteen, from any known sin. Sin is not in a place, and you can't get away from it. Sin is in the individual.

In this chapter we will look at the root of all human problems. The great majority of theologians talk about original sin. The fact is, there's nothing original about sin!

Think about that for a moment: There's nothing original about sin.

What is the worst thing you've ever done in your life? Or what have you done in the past month that you would label sinful? What led you to do that? Do you think you are the first person ever to act, feel, or relate in the fashion you are labeling sinful? There's nothing *original* about sin.

Augustine is one of the premier theologians of all times. In his classic book, *Confessions,* he told the story of his youthful escapade of stealing pears from a neighbor's tree. He recorded that late one night a group of youngsters went out to shake down and rob the tree. They took great loads of fruit from it "not for our own eating but rather to throw to the pigs." He went on to berate himself for the depth of sin this revealed. "The fruit gathered, I threw away, devouring in it only iniquity. There was no other reason, but foul was the evil, and I loved it."

Why would a harmless prank such as this one loom so large in Augustine's mind? By his own admission, he had taken a mistress, fathered a child out of wedlock, and indulged in every fleshly passion. Surely, any of these was more serious than stealing pears.

Augustine saw in the "pear incident" his true nature and the nature of all humankind: In each of us there is sin. Some would soften this and say that within each of us there is the *susceptibility* to sin. But Wesley, in the train of Paul and

37

Augustine, would say sin is there—not just a proneness to it, but sin itself. Since Adam, sin has been a part of every human life.

In this chapter, we will deal with the issue of original sin. But also, in light of the preceding chapters on salvation by faith, and prevenient grace and justifying grace, we will look at two other core concerns of a Wesleyan Christian: predestination and freedom, and regeneration and the new birth.

SIN IS UNIVERSAL

John Wesley talked more about the *universality* of sin than he did about original sin. I think he did this because he was not willing to go as far as Augustine, for instance, on the total depravity of human nature. But he wasn't far from that position. He believed in "total depravity," but as Gilbert Rowe put it, not in "tee-total depravity" because of his emphasis on grace. That's the reason we dealt with grace in the preceding chapter.

Recall that we said grace is universal, not limited. In Wesley's words, grace is "free in all, and free for all." About that there was no question. Wesley was as pessimistic about human nature as one could be, but there was a kind of optimism in his pessimism. Somewhere I saw a cartoon of a bum sitting on a park bench; his clothes were tattered and torn, his toes were coming out of his shoes—the stereotypical hobo. Beneath the picture was the caption: "No man is completely worthless—he can always serve as a horrible example."

Wesley knew himself and all human beings to be sinners; and we need to come to grips with that. But—and this is the rhythm and balance that is unique to Wesleyan theology—he was optimistic about grace. God's grace is sufficient. The power of sin is overcome by the power of God's love, mercy, and forgiveness. So John Wesley would join in the joyful triumphant cry of the apostle Paul: "Where sin increased, grace abounded all the more" (Rom. 5:20). Because of prevenient grace, universally bestowed by God, our freedom to respond to God is always guaranteed. We'll come back to this in a moment; for now, let's return to sin. (I don't mean that literally, though that is the human pattern; we're constantly returning to sin!)

Have you read about the small town of Centralia, Pennsylvania? It's a mining town. More than twenty years ago, a fire broke out in the labyrinthian maze of tunnels and shafts that honeycombs the earth beneath the town. First local, then state, and now federal mine officials have tried to put the fire out. They have done everything they know, but it just keeps burning. Now and then a puff of smoke will break through the surface just to let everyone know the fire is still there.

Sin is like that. It is not always rampant in our lives, though it often is. It's there—and there's nothing original about it.

The text for Wesley's sermon on original sin was Genesis 6:5: "The LORD saw that the wickedness of man was great in the earth, and that every imagination of the thoughts of his heart was only evil continually." Wesley laid the foundation for his sermon on original sin by sweeping quotations from Scripture:

39

> The Scripture avers, that "by one man's disobedience all men were constituted sinners"; that "in Adam, all died," spiritually died, lost the life and image of God; that fallen, sinful Adam then "begat a son in his own likeness"—nor was it possible he should beget him in any other; for "who can bring a clean thing out of unclean?"—That consequently we, as well as other men, were by nature "dead in trespasses and sin, without hope, without God in the world," and, therefore, "children of wrath"; that every man may say, "I was shapen in wickedness, and in sin did my mother conceive me"; that "there is no difference," in that "all have sinned and come short of the glory of God," of that glorious image of God wherein man was originally created. And hence, when the Lord

looked down from heaven upon the children of men, He saw they were all gone out of the way; that they were altogether become abominable, there was none righteous, no, not one, "none that truly sought after God."[1]

The Scripture passage with which we began this chapter is no isolated word from Paul. It is the witness of Scripture that with anguish Paul poured out a personal confession. Is there a more poignant expression of the civil war raging within? "For I know that nothing good dwells within me, that is, in my flesh. I can will what is right, but I cannot do it. . . . Wretched man that I am! Who will deliver me from this body of death?" (Rom. 7:18, 24). What a raging fire of conscience! What a gripping heartcry! How often do we feel that ripping inside, the tearing apart of our efforts to be whole and centered and headed in a clear direction!

It is not only a personal problem; it happens in the whole of society. During World War I, Karl Barth was the pastor of a village church in Switzerland. A great darkness had descended upon Europe. Seemingly, all the lights had gone out. Barth's people were crying for some word from the Lord that would make sense out of what had happened. Barth, however, had been raised in the nineteenth century and trained in its optimistic humanism; therefore, he had nothing to preach. In desperation he turned to the Scripture and discovered what he called "the strange new world within the Bible." Out of that experience, he wrote a book entitled *The Word of God and the Word of Man*. What Barth found in the Bible was strange because it described a world unlike the image of the world held by the confident liberals of the nineteenth century. When he came to Paul's Letter to the Romans, Barth found there a diagnosis of the human condition that offered a reason for the chaos of his time.

The beginning point for Paul is stark realism about sin. He rejects, out of hand, the idea that sin is something we can get rid of with proper upbringing, good education, healthy environment, or cultural growth and planned development of civilization. Sin is at the very heart of our lives—in fact, sin lies beneath the surface of our lives and penetrates to the very core. That's what we mean when we talk about original sin. And there's nothing original about it because we are all infected by it.

Don't be naive about sin in your life, Paul would say—and likewise, Wesley and the early Methodists. The duchess of Buckingham complained to the countess of Huntingdon about this radical doctrine of sin being preached by the early Methodist preachers, and she received this reply from the countess: "I thank your Ladyship for the information concerning the Methodist preachers. Their doctrines are most repulsive and strongly tinctured with impertinence and disrespect toward their superiors, in perpetually endeavoring to level all ranks and do away with all distinctions. It is monstrous to be told that you have a heart as sinful as the common wretches that crawl the earth."[2]

There are those in our day who still think it impertinent and repulsive to talk about sin in this fashion. For them, the problems of society and personal misery are located not in our alienation from God—not in our sin—but somewhere else. Our ignorance, not sin, is the problem. Psychological maladjustment, not sin, is our dilemma. Our surroundings are what "get to us"—not sin. Our feeling of powerlessness—not sin—is the reason we're so impotent in living effectively in the world. Economic inequities, limited education, the inequality among persons—not sin—are driving this country mad. So, if we improve education, if we cultivate self-understanding, if we raise everybody's standard of living, if we arrange proper socialization, people will be saved and will be happy and fulfilled. Evil will disappear, and the problems of the world will be solved.

We tend to want to leave sin to the rescue missions, to the fundamentalist sects, to TV evangelists. Sin doesn't fit in our enlightened age of self-actualization, social engineering, positive thinking, and the delusion of "I'm OK, you're OK."

I think Wesley would laugh at us. He insisted that belief

41

in a doctrine of universal sin is "the first distinguishing point between heathenism and Christianity. . . . Is man by nature filled with all manner of evil? Is he void of all good? Is he wholly fallen? Is his soul totally corrupted? . . . Allow this and you are so far a Christian. Deny it and you are heathen still."[3]

This is a grim picture, but the Gospels, the apostle Paul, and Wesley have a saving word for us. In his understanding of sin, Wesley took a position between the extreme of tee-total depravity—in which we are utterly and hopelessly sinful, the image of God within having been obliterated—and the naive contention that we are able to sin or not to sin as we choose. Wesley condemned the latter, the notion that we are able to sin or not sin as we please. Scripture and experience argued convincingly against the possibility that we can banish sin from our own lives and from society if we can simply muster up sufficient moral effort and courage.

But Wesley also refused to go to the other extreme of Calvin: That with the image of God within us obliterated, we are utterly and hopelessly sinful. Instead of seeing sin as an obliteration of the image of God within us, he saw it as a *malignant disease* that could be cured only by the powerful grace of God. And this brings us to talk about predestination and free will.

PREDESTINATION OR FREEDOM?

The extreme diagnosis of the human condition—that we are tee-totally depraved—has it that the image of God has been completely obliterated by Adam's fall. There is no way to change that. Thus comes the doctrine of *predestination* and *election*. Some are predestined to salvation by God's sovereign choice—and that is their only hope. For those who are not predestined to salvation—well, you know their fate.

Now here is a unique Wesleyan nuance: Wesley contended that the image of God in persons was not obliterated by the Fall; it was distorted, broken, obscured, crusted over with sin and self-will, but not obliterated. Sin was a malignant disease always portending death, apart from the miracle of God's grace.

Then came the second big difference. Wesley's understanding of "prevenient grace" and free will displaced the notion of election.

Calvin said, "We shall never be clearly convinced as we ought to be, that our salvation flows from the fountain of God's free mercy, till we are acquainted with his eternal election, which illustrates the grace of God by this comparison, that he adopts not all promiscuously to the hope of salvation, but gives to some what he refuses to others."[4]

For Calvin, predestination meant that God has once and for all determined, by immutable and eternal decree, all those who will be admitted to salvation and those who will be condemned to destruction. For him, justifying grace was restricted, limited, and particular. But not so with Wesley.

At the heart of Wesley's proclamation of the gospel was God's offer of grace to all. He felt that the doctrine of predestination was full of blasphemy. "Of such blasphemy," he said in his *Notes on The New Testament* "as I should dread to mention, but that the honor of our gracious God and the cause of truth will not suffer me to be silent."[5]

He argued from reason and experience, but primarily on the basis of Scripture. How can it be?

43

> This doctrine of predestination and election makes Jesus Christ a hypocrite, a deceiver of men, and a leader without honesty or ordinary sincerity. For it cannot be denied that Jesus everywhere speaks as if he is willing that all men should be saved. Listen to his pleas to the Jews in Matthew 23:37: "O Jerusalem, Jerusalem, killing the prophets and stoning those who are sent to you! How often would I have gathered your children together as a hen gathers her brood under her wings, and you would not!" His words are full of invitations to sinners: "Come to me, all who labor and are heavy laden, and I will give you rest" (Matt. 11:28). If you say that he did not intend to save all sinners, if you say he calls those that cannot

come, then you represent the Son of God as mocking his helpless creatures by offering what he never intends to give. You describe him as saying one thing and meaning another; as pretending the love which he had not, "Him, in whose mouth was no guile," you make full of deceit, void of common sincerity."[6]

Wesley was vehemently opposed to a doctrine of predestination and election because he felt it affected the whole of Christian belief and experience. The most obvious thing the doctrine of predestination does is to make preaching vain. Of what value is preaching to those who, with or without it, will be infallibly saved? And is preaching not a mockery to those who are not elected? They cannot understand or respond. To offer false hope to people who are damned already is a cruel charade.

But more than making preaching vain, the doctrine of predestination is, as Bishop Cannon reminds us,

> no doctrine of God, for it directly tends to destroy holiness, which is the end of all the ordinances of God. It takes away those first motives of holiness, which are the hope of future reward and the fear of punishment.
>
> Immediately the Calvinist replies, "But man knows not whether he is assigned to life or death." Wesley answers that such knowledge is beside the point, and then makes this famous remark:
>
> "If a sick man knows that he must unavoidably die, or unavoidably recover, though he knows not which, it is unreasonable for him to take any physic at all. He might justly say (and so I have heard some speak, both in bodily sickness and spiritual), 'If I am ordained to life, I shall live; if to death, I shall die; so I need not trouble myself about it.' "[7]

Wesley argued that predestination tends to destroy the comforts of religion as well as any zeal for good works. But Wesley's big claim was that predestination overthrows the whole Christian revelation of who God is as we see the Eternal in Jesus Christ. In his sometimes extreme way of putting things, Wesley said the doctrine pictures God as worse than the Devil, more *false, unjust,* and *cruel.*

> More *false;* because the devil, liar as he is, hath never said, "He willeth all men to be saved." More *unjust;* because the devil cannot, if he would, be guilty of such an injustice as you ascribe to God, when you say that God condemned millions of souls to everlasting fire, prepared for the devil and his angels, for continuing sin for want of that grace *he will not* give them, they cannot avoid. And more *cruel;* because that unhappy spirit "seeketh rest and findeth none"; so that his own restless misery is a kind of temptation to him to tempt others. But God resteth in his high and holy place; so that to suppose him, of his own mere motion, of his pure will and pleasure, happy as he is, to doom his creatures, whether they will or no, to endless misery, is to impute such cruelty to him as we cannot impute even to the great enemy of God and Man."[8]

If we had to select a single gospel message to present the essence of God's intention for us, wouldn't it be that text from John 3:16–17? "For God so loved the world that he gave his only Son, that whoever believes in him should not perish but have eternal life. For God sent the Son into the world, not to condemn the world, but that the world might be saved through him." There's nothing exclusive or limited about that.

So, we Wesleyans contend with John Wesley that sin is universal, but that grace is free in all and free for all, that whosoever will, may come.

REGENERATION IS REQUIRED

Since sin is universal and is a malignant disease in our lives, to use a medical image, radical surgery is essential to deal with it. *Regeneration*—a new birth—is required. Not only are we forgiven, not only are we reconciled to God, but we are made new, regenerated. This is what the psalmist was pleading for: "Create in me a clean heart, O God, and put a new and right spirit within me" (Ps. 51:10). This is what Paul contended would happen to us: "If any one is in Christ, he is a new creation; the old has passed away, behold, the new has come" (2 Cor. 5:17).

The healing of the malignant disease of sin involves a threefold prescription: (1) repentance that flows from honest self-knowledge and includes genuine sorrow and remorse; (2) renunciation of self-will, a willingness to yield our wills to Christ since the will is the seat of sin; and (3) faith, which is a complete trust in God's sheer unmerited grace.

We are not helpless creatures, predestined to either eternal death or eternal life. We *are* free. We *do* participate in our salvation. We respond. When we finally come to ourselves and realize that we are sinners beyond hope of saving ourselves, that God's grace is for us, that God's unmerited love is not to be earned but to be received, we drop to our knees to receive our Redeemer in an embrace of faith and acceptance.

Here is a hint of it in the story of Benjamin West who tells us about how he became a painter. One day his mother went out, leaving him in charge of his little sister Sally. He discovered some bottles of colored ink and began to paint Sally's portrait. He really made a mess of things. Ink blots were all over. On her return, the mother saw the mess, but grace prevailed. She said nothing, picked up one piece of paper, and saw the drawing. "It's Sally," she said immediately and excitedly, and then gave Benjamin a kiss. Later, this great painter, Benjamin West, said, "My mother's kiss made me a painter."

God's kiss of grace makes us Christian. It is an extravagant grace that works within us, preveniently, preserving that last bit of freedom that is ours to respond to, working as unmerited love to justify us and account us as righteous even though we are sinners—to *regenerate* us, to give us new birth—and, finally, to *sanctify* us, making us new creatures. It is sanctifying grace that we will discuss in the next chapter.

Wesley closed his sermon on original sin with this word:

46

Keep to the plain old faith, "once delivered to the saints," and delivered by the Spirit of God to our hearts. Know your disease! Know your cure! You were born to sin: therefore, "you must be born again," born of God. By nature ye are wholly corrupted: by grace ye shall be wholly renewed. In Adam, ye all died: in the second Adam, in Christ, ye all are made alive. "You that were dead in sins hath He quickened": He hath already given you a principle of life, even faith in Him who loved you and gave Himself for you! Now "go on from faith to faith," until your whole sickness be healed, and all that "mind be in you which was also in Christ Jesus"![9]

To that, I only add that redeemed by Christ, we will continue to sing in awe:

> And can it be that I should gain
>   An interest in the Savior's blood?
> Died he for me, who caused his pain?
>   For me, who him to death pursued?
> Amazing love! how can it be
>   That thou, my Lord, shouldst die for me?[10]

4
"But No One Can Be Perfect!" Who Says?

For this is the will of God, your sanctification: that you abstain from unchastity (1 Thess. 4:3).

For God has not called us for uncleanness, but in holiness (1 Thess. 4:7).

For I am the LORD who brought you up out of the land of Egypt, to be your God; you shall therefore be holy, for I am holy (Lev. 11:45).

You, therefore, must be perfect, as your heavenly Father is perfect (Matt. 5:48).

Let those of us who are mature be thus minded; and if in anything you are otherwise minded, God will reveal that also to you (Phil. 3:15).

The idea of my writing a chapter on Christian perfection may appear to those who know me like proposing to write a book with the title, *Humility and How I Attained It*. Even so, it must be done, for Wesley viewed Christian perfection as the *grand depositum* of Methodism.

We are returning to pick up Wesley's theme of grace. In chapter 2 we discussed *prevenient* grace and *justifying* grace. Now to complete the trilogy, we will discuss *sanctifying* grace. Our attention may be riveted on the theme by thinking about perfection, for that is what sanctifying grace is all about:

Christian perfection. Thus the title of this chapter: " 'But No One Can Be Perfect!' Who Says?"

Wesley believed that God had raised up the people called Methodists to keep asking the question, "Who says?"—and to do this by claiming and proclaiming the scriptural call to holiness of heart and life.

We could have chosen any number of Scripture passages to undergird this chapter, for the Bible is full of injunctions to perfection, to purity of heart and life—to holiness. God put the call clearly in Leviticus 11:45. And Jesus put it as clearly in His Sermon on the Mount. Wesley said it this way: "Ye know that the great end of religion is, to renew our hearts in the image of God, to repair this total loss of righteousness and true holiness which we sustained by the sin of our first parents."[1]

Interestingly, Wesley chose Philippians 3:12 for the text of his basic sermon on Christian perfection. You remember this verse as Paul's word about his own life: "Not that I have already obtained this or am already perfect."

That may seem to be an argument against perfection; but in his introduction to the sermon, Wesley reminded his hearers and readers that immediately after Paul's disclaimer, he made a specific claim in verse 15: "Let us therefore," he said, "as many as be perfect, be thus minded" (KJV). This seeming conflict in Paul's claim is a clear call to seek understanding of what we mean when we talk about sanctification, holiness, or Christian perfection. All three point to the same work of grace in our lives—sanctifying grace.

Let us then seek clarity about the meaning of sanctification, this central Wesleyan doctrine. To do so, we must review a bit. To picture the idea of salvation, Wesley used the image of a house. Repentance was the porch; justification was the entry door; and all the rooms in the house were facets of our sanctification. It all begins with repentance—when we are convinced and convicted of our sins, are genuinely sorry, and accept by faith what God has done for us in Jesus Christ. When we respond in faith to God's grace, we are justified,

49

made right with God, not because of our merit, but by divine grace. *Justification* is another word for pardon. Therefore, justification is what God does *for* us. That brings us to our focus: Sanctification, which is what God does *in* us. As Albert Outler would remind us: "In justification we *gain* God's favor; holy-living is the life-process in which we seek to *retain* it [that favor]."[2]

On the surface, Outler's explanation seems to imply *sanctification by works*. Not so in Wesley's understanding. We are not justified by grace and sanctified by works. We are both saved and sanctified by grace.

It will help us to realize that salvation, then, is a process—a process that begins with justification but continues as we grow in grace toward sanctification, which is the goal of our salvation. Sanctifying grace is the work of Christ within us—Christ's Spirit restoring the broken image, completing what was begun in justification.

A division occurred in the Wesleyan family in the nineteenth century, moving this doctrine of sanctification from the mainstream into an eddy that has been stirred only now and then by the Wesleyan movement. It began in a most promising way, as a revival of emphasis on holiness began to move through the church. But, as is so often the case, people began to preach a particularized experience as the norm. Doctrines were rigidly defined. A big segment of the church objected strenuously to some evangelists' particular ideas about holiness, and especially rejected a notion of "second blessing sanctification." (At the risk of oversimplification, I will say that the doctrine of "second blessing sanctification" claimed that in a second experience of grace—like that operative in conversion or justification—an individual's carnal nature might be eradicated so that the person could live a sinless life.) Unfortunately, for some the doctrine was "cast in concrete," rigidly and tenaciously presented as the standard for Christian living.

We must not let the extreme rigidity of certain people blind us to the possibility of sanctification, even entire sanctification. Wesley's Aldersgate experience convinced him that sanctification, like justification, was granted in an instant. We fail to do justice to Wesley if we do not recognize that in his growth and teaching he changed. We do not give Wesley's hallmark doctrine of sanctification its full due unless we see it as a dynamic, not a static thing.

Sanctification comes both in a moment and as a lifelong process. We are born into sanctification (by grace); then we grow in it by grace. Some outstanding Wesleyan scholars teach and profess the full eradication of sin. I long for this, but have not experienced it myself. Wesley preached sermons on sin and repentance in believers; yet he stated clearly that many of those who are sanctified are no longer tempted.

The division in the Wesleyan family in the nineteenth century was fired by the reaction of many people who, being unable to harmonize the truth about perfection and holiness with their experienced reality, "threw the baby out with the bathwater." Rejecting what they considered to be an altogether too narrow definition of sanctification or holiness, and fleeing from an obvious stance of self-righteousness, they went to the opposite extreme. They forgot sanctification altogether. For some time, few people within the mainstream of the United Methodist Church have attempted to understand entire sanctification or live a life of true holiness.

Yet no reputable Wesleyan scholar denies that the teaching of holiness was one of Wesley's foremost contributions to an understanding of the Christian way. So, let's take a solid look at it:

With the Wesleyan family's varying emphases on the different aspects of sanctification, it is helpful to keep in mind Wesley's *order of sanctification*. He taught that sanctification is a process/moment/process. Some will argue, with good support from Wesley, that entire sanctification is the beginning point of the process. But this does not preclude a process of spiritual growth preceding the *moment* of entire sanctification. Wesley's understanding of grace assumed that there could be such a moment. For, if God sanctifies a believer—

and God does—then God can do it in a moment. Even so, as prevenient grace leads a person to justification, sanctifying grace leads to the moment of entire sanctification. Then the process continues—process/moment/process.

To get a clearer understanding of this, let's consider (1) what Christian perfection is not, (2) what Christian perfection is, and (3) what sanctifying grace does in our lives.

PERFECTION IS NOT . . .

First, let's examine what Christian perfection is not.

Christian perfection is not freedom from ignorance. The Bible and Wesley are very clear about this. Sanctifying grace does not turn us into superhuman robots, computerized and controlled by God to think and perform in a rigidly regulated way. No, we will always be limited in our wisdom and understanding. We will always "see through a glass darkly"— until that happy day in the kingdom when the scales will be removed from our eyes, and we will see clearly and know even as we are known.

If Christian perfection means that we will never in this life be free of ignorance and lack of understanding, it certainly follows that *we will not be free of error or mistake.* John Wesley put a proviso on this one. He said,

> It is true, the children of God do not mistake as to the things essential to salvation: they do not "put darkness for light, or light for darkness"; neither "seek death at the error of their life." For they are "taught of God"; and the way which he teaches them, the way of holiness, is so plain, that "the wayfaring man, though a fool, need not err therein." But in things unessential to salvation they do err, and that frequently.[3]

Wesley wanted to leave no excuse for the superficial notion that we do not know enough to be saved or that we do not know enough to live a holy life.

52

I'm especially impressed by what Wesley said about interpretation of Scripture, for this has been the cause for schism in the church throughout our history. Listen to him:

> Nay, with regard to the holy Scriptures themselves, as careful as they are to avoid it, the best of men are liable to mistake, and do mistake day by day; especially with respect to those parts thereof which less immediately relate to practice. Hence, even the children of God are not agreed as to the interpretation of many places in holy writ; nor is their difference of opinion any proof that they are not the children of God, on either side; but it is proof that we are no more to expect any living man to be infallible, than to be omniscient.[4]

The third thing Christian perfection is not is *freedom from infirmities*. Again, we need to be clear about the meaning. By speaking of "infirmities," Wesley was not giving anyone an out to sin—in fact, he warned against giving this "soft title to known sins." Let Wesley give his conviction on this thought:

> So, one man tells us, "Every man has his infirmity, and mine is drunkenness"; another has the infirmity of uncleanness; another, that of taking God's holy name in vain; and yet another has the infirmity of calling his brother, "Thou fool" or returning "railing for railing." It is plain that all you who thus speak, if ye repent not, shall, with your infirmities go quick to hell! But I mean hereby, not only those which are properly termed *bodily infirmities*, but all those inward or outward imperfections which are not of a moral nature.[5]

The last thing Christian perfection is not is *freedom from temptation*. "Such freedom from temptation belongeth not to this life." Wesley had a marvelous way of challenging complacency and shattering self-righteous images. In the matter of temptation he said of those who were satisfied with a form of godliness they were practicing: "There are also many whom the wise enemy of souls seeing to be fast asleep in the dead form of godliness, will not tempt to gross sin, lest they should awake before they drop into everlasting burnings."[6]

As he dealt with such self-righteous people harshly, he dealt with others tenderly:

> I know there are also children of God who, being now justified freely, having found redemption in the blood of Christ, for the present feel no temptation. God hath said to their enemies, "Touch not Mine anointed, and do My children no harm." And for this season, it may be weeks or months, He causes them to ride on high places, He beareth them on eagles' wings, above all the fiery darts of the wicked one. But this state will not last always; as we may learn from that single consideration, that the Son of God Himself, in the days of His flesh, was tempted even to the end of His life.[7]

Let me reiterate. Christian perfection is not freedom or exemption from ignorance, mistakes, infirmities, or temptation.

PERFECTION IS . . .

Now let us consider what Christian perfection is. This requires looking at the whole picture of salvation as Wesley perceived it in Scripture and experience.

Wesley placed a strong emphasis on regeneration or the new birth as distinguished from justification. Many Christian thinkers do not make this distinction, but Wesley had a clear picture of what he called the "order of salvation" in which he stated the difference.

He used the text from John 3:7, "You must be born anew," for his sermon "The New Birth." He began that sermon saying,

> If any doctrines within the whole compass of Christianity may be properly termed "fundamental," they are doubtless these two—the doctrine of justification, and that of the new birth: the former relating to that great work

which God does *for us,* in forgiving our sins; the latter, to the great work which God does *in us,* in renewing our fallen nature.[8]

Though distinctive, the doctrines of justification and new birth belong together. God acts for us to forgive us and begins the restoration of the divine image within us at the same time. This is the reason the new birth is such a powerful image. As physical birth is the momentous beginning of physical life on earth, new birth in Christ is the beginning of a life of the soul for spiritual growth. We are by God's grace redeemed from sin, justified in relation to Him. We are also born of the Spirit. Wesley defined the nature of the new birth in this fashion:

> It is that great change which God works in the soul when He brings it into life; when He raises it from the death of sin to the life of righteousness. It is the change wrought in the whole soul by the almighty Spirit of God when it is "created anew in Christ Jesus"; when it is "renewed after the image of God in righteousness and true holiness"; when the love of the world is changed into the love of God; pride into humility; passion into meekness; hatred, envy, malice, into a sincere, tender, disinterested love for all mankind.[9]

55

In a word, it is that change whereby the earthly, sensual, devilish mind is turned into the mind which was in Christ Jesus (see Phil. 2:5). This is the nature of the new birth: "so it is with every one that is born of the Spirit" (John 3:8).

Now stay with me. I'm not being picky; this is crucial. There is a distinction between God's action *for* the sinner (pardon and justification) and God's action *in* the pardoned sinner's heart (restoration of the broken image and of the human power to avoid and resist intentional sin). Albert Outler puts it this way: "We have no part in our justification before God, save the passive act of accepting and trusting the merits of Christ. But we have a crucial part to play in the further business of 'growing up into Christ, into the stature of the perfect man.'"[10]

It is easy to get confused because the point is subtle. We must remember that we seek sanctification by grace, just as we seek justification by grace. Grace opens the door, and by grace we walk through it. God does not say, "I saved you, now live up to it." God saves us and then empowers us to live up to the fullness of salvation. It's the difference between obeying the law of sin and death, and obeying the law of the Spirit of life.

> There is therefore now no condemnation for those who are in Christ Jesus. For the law of the Spirit of life in Christ Jesus has set me free from the law of sin and death. For God has done what the law, weakened by the flesh, could not do: sending his own Son in the likeness of sinful flesh and for sin, he condemned sin in the flesh, in order that the just requirement of the law might be fulfilled in us, who walk not according to the flesh but according to the Spirit (Rom. 8:1–4).

This is important to grasp, because here again I believe we witness the genius of John Wesley in bringing harmony to an understanding of the gospel. Let me illustrate, I hope without being judgmental.

Albert Outler reminds us that in a strict fundamentalist theology there is a preoccupation with the work of Christ for our salvation and an unhealthy indifference to human responsibility in the struggle for God's justice in human society. On the other hand, the stereotypical liberal has a well-defined social agenda and is ardently committed to the kingdom issues of peace and justice. But unfortunately, there is little emphasis in the so-called liberal camp on the foundation on which the kingdom is established, that is, God's personal salvation in Jesus Christ. So Outler concludes:

> The liberal speaks easily of Christ as revealer and exemplar but tends to stammer when pressed back toward any evangelical notions of mediatorial sacrifice. This is why neither fundamentalists nor liberals have a more than tenuous hold on the *full* Christian tradition, as

we have seen Wesley trying to put it together and hold it together. Wesleyans, in his train, have a less than impressive record in doing this as well as he did.[11]

Is it clear? Wesley put equal emphasis on justification and regeneration or the new birth. Both are works of the grace of God in our lives. In justification, we are pardoned and reconciled to God. In regeneration, the restoration of the image of God is begun. And that brings us to sanctification.

Sanctification is not to be confused with justification or the new birth. Justification and the new birth may be the miracle of a moment, but sanctification is the task of a lifetime. For some believers, sanctification is a process leading to an experience of entire sanctification. For others, it is a process leading to many experiences, in a never-ending adventure whereby the grace of God works out in fact what is already true in principle.

In *position*, in our relationship to God in Jesus Christ, we are new persons; that is justification and the new birth. Now our *condition*, the actual life that we live, must be brought into harmony with our new position. That is the process of sanctification.

Justification, the new birth, is the starting point of sanctification. "It is the gate to it, the entrance to it," Wesley said.

57

> When we are born again, then our sanctification, our reward and outward holiness begins; and thence forward we are, gradually to "grow up in Him who is our Head." This expression of the Apostle admirably illustrates the difference between one and the other, and further points out the exact analogy there is between natural and spiritual things. A child is born of a woman in a moment, or at least in a very short time: afterward he gradually and slowly grows, til he attains the stature of a man. In like manner, a child is born of God in a short time, if not in a moment. But it is by slow degrees that he afterward grows up to the measure of the full stature of Christ.[12]

So, what is sanctification? It is, in Paul's words, growing up into human maturity, "to the measure of the stature of the fulness of Christ" (Eph. 4:13). It is, again in Paul's words, "until Christ be formed in you" (Gal. 4:19). It is a total response to Jesus' call: "Take my yoke upon you, and learn from me" (Matt. 11:29). It is Jesus' promise to abide in us if we will abide in Him.

Two phrases will help us in understanding Christian perfection: *singleness of intention* and *perfection in love*. I heard of a young man who received a letter from his ex-fiancée, which read as follows: "Dear John: Words cannot express the deep regret I feel at having broken our engagement. Will you take me back? Your absence leaves me empty and no one else will ever fill the void. Please forgive me and let us start again. I love you. I love you. I love you. Your adoring Sally. P.S. Congratulations on winning the Irish Sweepstakes." I'd say her motives, intention, and love were less than pure!

One of the chief characteristics of Christian perfection is the willingness to be transformed by the Holy Spirit. Kierkegaard reminded us that "purity of heart is to will one thing."

But how can our intention be called "single" and our love be called "perfect" while we know that we are obviously flawed? Steve Harper has provided a very clear illustration from parenting that gives us a clue. He writes:

> When each of my own children were small, they had the bright idea to bring mommy some flowers. Never mind that they plucked the flowers from the bed mommy had worked hard to cultivate. Never mind that they might have even taken flowers from their neighbor's bed! Their one desire was to please mommy and to show their love for her. So, in they came with flowers, weeds, and dirt. With faces aglow, they exclaimed, "Mommy, we love you!"
>
> What did mommy do? Did she throw the flowers away because they had clumps of weeds and grass clinging to them? Did she refuse to accept them because they were

pulled from her bed or the bed of a neighbor? Of course not! She saw the deed through the eyes of love, took her nicest vase, and proudly displayed the flowers on the table. She accepted the act of love, even though she might follow it (at an appropriate time) with a lesson in flower-picking.

So it is with God. He accepts our intentions. He sees our motives. It has to be this way, for in the light of his impeccable holiness even our best actions fall short. The Bible puts it this way: even our best actions look like filthy rags in comparison to God. We cannot hope to match him in actions, but we can be one with him in motive. Our controlling desire can be to do his will on earth as it is in heaven. God knows whether or not that is our intention, and when it is, he calls it "perfect" even though it comes packaged with some weeds and dirt.[13]

SANCTIFYING GRACE AT WORK

Now we move to the third consideration: What does sanctifying grace do for us?

First, it *gives us power over sin*. Wesley was rooted in Scripture here, especially in Paul. "Consider yourselves dead to sin and alive to God in Christ Jesus," Paul said in Romans 6:11. No longer are we to be "enslaved to sin," he contended in Romans 6:6. Settle this truth clearly in your mind. In any given situation, God's grace is more powerful than the lure of temptation. *Sanctifying grace gives us power over sin.*

Second, sanctifying grace *equips us for ministry*. To be *holy* is to be "set apart." One of the biblical meanings of *sanctification* is to be "consecrated for the services of God." God said, "For I am the LORD your God; consecrate yourselves therefore, and be holy, for I am holy" (Lev. 11:44).

The call to sanctification is a personal call to holiness, but it is also a social imperative. (We will consider this more fully in chapter 7, "Holiness of Heart and Life." I like the way someone introduced Mother Theresa: "She gave her life first to Christ, and then through Christ to her neighbor. That was the end of her biography, and the beginning of her life." Sanctifying grace equips us for ministry.

Finally, *sanctifying grace provides us an experience in which we can grow.* Sanctification is not static. When we talk about sanctification, we're not talking about "sinless perfection." Wesley himself did not use that phrase. Christians do not commit *willful* sins. If they do, they lose God's favor—we call that "backsliding." The impulse and power of sin are not destroyed in justification or regeneration. Wesley would say they are suspended. Sin is *present*, but it does not *prevail* in our lives. So Charles Wesley would sing his prayer: "Take away our bent to sinning." This bent to sin, the possibility that is lurking there, must be dealt with by daily repentance, daily spiritual disciplines, daily renewals of faith, and daily exercises of love until we have singleness of intention and are perfected in love. We too sing it:

> *Finish, then, thy new creation;*
> *Pure and spotless let us be.*
> *Let us see thy great salvation*
> *Perfectly restored in thee:*
> *Changed from glory into glory,*
> *Till in heaven we take our place,*
> *Till we cast our crowns before thee,*
> *Lost in wonder, love, and praise.*[14]

That's the work of sanctifying grace. It gives us power over sin; it equips us for ministry; it gives us an experience in which we can grow.

There is a marvelous story out of the life of George Matheson, one of the renowned preachers of Scotland in another generation, that gives us a "feel" for what sanctification means. When he came to one of the great Presbyterian churches in Edinburgh, there was a woman in the congregation who lived in filthy conditions in a cellar. After some months of Matheson's ministry, it came time for Communion in the life of the church. In the Scottish

Presbyterian tradition, elders call on members of the congregation to sign them up for Communion. When the elder called at this woman's cellar with the card, he found her gone. After much effort, he tracked her down, finally locating her in an attic room. She was very poor; there were no luxuries. But the attic was as light and airy and clean as the cellar had been dark and dismal and dirty.

"I see you've changed your house," the elder said to the woman.

"Aye," she said, "I have. You canna' hear George Matheson preach and live in a cellar."

That's the picture of sanctifying grace: "Changed from glory into glory" until we know singleness of intention and perfection in love. "Changed from glory into glory, / Till in heaven we take our place."

The benediction of Paul is a blessing and a call to Christian perfection: "May the God of peace himself sanctify you wholly; and may your spirit and soul and body be kept sound and blameless at the coming of our Lord Jesus Christ. He who calls you is faithful, and he will do it" (1 Thess. 5:23–24).

61

5
Assurance:
The Privilege of
All Believers

There is therefore now no condemnation for those who are in Christ Jesus. For the law of the Spirit of life in Christ Jesus has set me free from the law of sin and death. For God has done what the law, weakened by the flesh, could not do: sending his own Son in the likeness of sinful flesh and for sin, he condemned sin in the flesh, in order that the just requirement of the law might be fulfilled in us, who walk not according to the flesh but according to the Spirit. For those who live according to the flesh set their minds on the things of the flesh, but those who live according to the Spirit set their minds on the things of the Spirit. . . . Any one who does not have the Spirit of Christ does not belong to him. But if Christ is in you, although your bodies are dead because of sin, your spirits are alive because of righteousness. If the Spirit of him who raised Jesus from the dead dwells in you, he who raised Christ Jesus from the dead will give life to your mortal bodies also through his Spirit which dwells in you. So then, brethren, we are debtors, not to the flesh, to live according to the flesh—for if you live according to the flesh you will die, but if by the Spirit you put to death the deeds of the body you will live. For all who are led by the Spirit of God are sons of God. For you did not receive the spirit of slavery to fall back into fear, but you have received the spirit of sonship. When we cry, "Abba! Father!" it is the Spirit himself bearing witness with our spirit that we are children of God, and if children, then heirs, heirs of God and fellow heirs with Christ, provided we suffer with him in order that we may also be glorified with him (Rom. 8:1–5, 9–17).

One of my favorite writers is Loren Eiseley. He was an anthropologist and naturalist who blended scientific knowledge and imaginative vision. He recorded his findings with the perception of a painter, the words of a poet, and the heart of a prophet. Here is one of his powerful personal reflections:

The sound that awoke me was the outraged cries of the nestling's parents, who flew helplessly in circles about the clearing. [A raven had raided their home to eat the babies.] The sleek black monster was indifferent to them. He gulped, whetted his beak on the dead branch a moment and sat still. Up to that point, the little tragedy had followed the usual pattern. But suddenly, out of all that area of woodland, a soft sound of complaint began to rise. Into the glade fluttered small birds of half a dozen varieties drawn by the anguished outcries of the tiny parents.

. . . There, in that clearing, the crystal note of a song sparrow lifted hesitantly in the hush. And finally, after painful fluttering, another took the song, and then another, the song passing from one bird to another, doubtfully at first, as though some evil thing were being slowly forgotten. . . . In simple truth, they had forgotten the raven, for they were the singers of life, and not of death.[1]

That's a lesson from nature about two Christian realities that were distinctively emphasized by John Wesley: assurance, which is the privilege of all believers, set in the grim reality of sin, which can and often does persist in the life of the believer.

Loren Eiseley's story is a bridge between our discussion of sanctification in the last chapter and our theme of assurance in this chapter. The birds "sang under the brooding shadow of the raven. In simple truth, they had forgotten the raven, for

63

they were the singers of life, and not of death." It is a revealing image of the style of a Christian. How beautifully and powerfully did Paul express it in Romans 8. Focus again on his claims.

Verse 2: "For the law of the Spirit of life in Christ Jesus has set me free from the law of sin and death."

Verse 5: "For those who live according to the flesh set their minds on the things of the flesh, but those who live according to the Spirit set their minds on the things of the Spirit."

Verses 15–16: "For you did not receive the spirit of slavery to fall back into fear, but you have received the spirit of sonship. When we cry, 'Abba! Father!' it is the Spirit himself bearing witness with our spirit that we are children of God."

To be true to our situation, we have to admit one fallacy in the image. The birds may have forgotten the raven as they sang; the Christian sings, but does not forget the raven. *The presence of sin and evil is always an ominous awareness for the Christian. Sin abounds—but the Christian sings—because grace does much more abound!*

So we must consider sin in the life of the believer and then move on to talk about the song-inspiring gospel of assurance, which is a central belief of a Wesleyan Christian.

POWER OVER SIN

First, let's talk about sin in the life of the believer. Does even the possibility of sin sound completely out of sync with the Wesleyan teaching on Christian perfection, reviewed in the last chapter? Well, it does, and that's the reason we must face it head on.

We affirmed in the last chapter that one of Wesley's primary claims was that sanctifying grace *gives us power over sin*. Recall what we emphasized about that point. Paul said in Romans 6:11: "Consider yourselves dead to sin and alive to God in Christ Jesus." In the Scripture quoted at the beginning of this chapter, Paul contended that "the law of the Spirit of life in Christ Jesus has set me free from the law of sin and death."

One of the strongest tenets of Wesley's theology is that God's grace—His regenerative and sanctifying grace—keeps us so long as we keep it. In Romans 8, Paul used the terms *flesh* and *Spirit* to designate our dual nature. In the seventh chapter of Romans, he shared his own classic witness of the conflict that continues to rage in the life of the Christian: "For I do not do the good I want, but the evil I do not want is what I do. . . . Wretched man that I am!" (vv. 19, 24).

In Galatians 5:17, Paul put it this way: "For the desires of the flesh are against the Spirit, and the desires of the Spirit are against the flesh; for these are opposed to each other, to prevent you from doing what you would."

Paul wrote to the believers in Corinth and addressed them as those "sanctified in Christ Jesus" (1 Cor. 1:2). Yet he said: "I, brethren, could not address you as spiritual men, but as men of the flesh, as babes in Christ. . . . for you are still of the flesh" (1 Cor. 3:1, 3).

This Corinthian passage gives us a clear clue to understanding that sin persists in the life of the believer. The Corinthians were brothers and sisters in Christ with Paul, yet he saw sin in their lives. He identified their envy and strife, nevertheless he did not see them as having lost their faith.

Paul saw those persons in Corinth as babes in Christ. We need not get tied up with how long we may remain babes in Christ. To some degree, we may always be thus designated. But Paul and Wesley would not be cavalier about this. Sin, and our struggle against it, must always be seen as serious business. Wesley made the point clearly by asking the question: "But can Christ be in the same heart where sin is?" He responded: "Undoubtedly He can; otherwise it never could be saved therefrom." Where the sickness is, there is the Physician, "Carrying on His work within, / Striving till He cast out sin."[2]

He farther contended that "Christ indeed cannot *reign*

65

where sin reigns; neither will He dwell where any sin is *allowed*. But He *is* and *dwells* in the heart of every believer, who is *fighting against* all sin; although it be not yet purified, according to the purification of the sanctuary."[3]

Here is the truth in one sentence: Sin remains but no longer reigns in the Christian. Get that! Sin *remains* but no longer *reigns* in the Christian. We need to note this particular Wesleyan position because it is the foundation for Wesley's conflict with those who believe in eternal security, or what some Christians today label the doctrine of "once saved, always saved." Listen carefully to this succinct word of Wesley:

> A man may be in God's favour though he feels sins; but not if he *yields* to it. *Having sin* does not forfeit the favor of God; *giving way* to sin does. Though the flesh in you "lusts against the Spirit," you may still be a child of God; but if you "walk after the flesh," you are a child of the devil. Now this doctrine does not encourage one to obey sin, but to resist it with all our might.[4]

This is what separates our Wesleyan understanding of salvation from the popular belief in eternal security—we understand that our remaining saved depends on whether we yield to sin in our lives, to the point that we forfeit our salvation.

Thus it is not a question of whether God is able to keep us from falling. Of course God is able! It is a matter of whether we are constantly vigilant in responding to God's grace—whether we allow the Holy Spirit to sensitize our consciences, making us aware of the new sins that spring up in our lives and the sinful abuses of innocent human aspirations. Being kept by God depends on whether we will listen to God's voice and not allow that divine love to grow cold within us.

Let me restate the case by coming at it from a different direction. There are two widely held notions about sin in the believer that are different from Wesley's. One thought is that sin continues in the life of the believer, but it cannot separate that person eternally from God. According to this view, a person may backslide, but still be saved—if ever saved in the first place. This "if ever saved in the first place" provides a common explanation of why a professed Christian lapses into gross sin. We can say, "Well, the person was never saved anyway!" But how can we make that arbitrary judgment?

The second thought is that sin is completely eradicated from the believer's life. The error in this position is that it treats sin as an objective "thing." Wesley pointed out that sin is not a substance, but a relationship. The question is not whether sin has been *removed* from our lives, but whether we are *reconciled* with God.

According to Wesley, the new birth is the coming together again of a person and God. God's justifying grace makes this possible, and sanctifying grace is the continuation of the restorative process until we are so at one with God that our intentions are single (to do God's will) and our love is perfect (to love as Christ loves).

When we talk about sanctifying grace giving us power over sin—and what seems to be an opposite point, that there may be sin in the life of the believer—we must have a clear understanding of what we mean by sin. Wesley saw it as "an actual, voluntary transgression of the law; . . . acknowledged to be such at the time it is transgressed."[5] Wesley always left open the possibility of involuntary sin, which he felt did not bring God's condemnation. But to sin willfully in a continuous way certainly jeopardizes our salvation, for it separates us from God.

That case was clear for Wesley. We *may* "fall from grace" and forfeit our justification, but we don't *have* to. Whether we can or can't fall is not as important a question as whether we do or don't.

We must be aware of two major spiritual principles when we first become Christians: (1) the principle of the abiding potentiality of evil within our lives—the old sinful nature that remains latent even in regenerate persons, and (2) the principle of our absolute dependency on God. Even after we have

67

been converted, we can do no good by ourselves, but must rely completely on the Spirit of God, who performs the good in us and through us.

We must give ourselves to moral and spiritual discipline. As Christians, we repent daily and cast ourselves on God's grace. We grow in that grace and move from the threshold of faith—our justification by God—toward the fullness of grace, our sanctification. And all along the Christian way, we can be kept from falling from grace, kept from forfeiting our just-ification, by the glorious assurance of our salvation. Fanny Crosby wrote the lyric, but it's great Wesleyan theology:

> *Blessed assurance, Jesus is mine!*
> *O what a foretaste of glory divine!*
> *Heir of salvation, purchase of God,*
> *Born of His Spirit, washed in His blood.*[6]

And the third verse of that hymn states it clearly: "Perfect submission, all is at rest; / I in my Savior am happy and blest. . . ."

WESLEY AT ALDERSGATE

68

That leads to the primary focus of this chapter: *assurance.* Wesley's favorite text for this, one of the central themes of his theology, was Romans 8:16: "The Spirit himself bearing witness with our spirit that we are children of God."

Early in his ministry, Wesley taught that there was no authentic salvation without assurance. By the mid-1740s he had modified his position, believing no longer that assurance was necessary for salvation, but that it was the "common privilege of all believers." Wesley testified to this change in an interesting letter to Mr. Melville Horne. He wrote: "When fifty years ago my brother Charles and I, in the simplicity of our hearts, told the good people of England that unless they knew their sins were forgiven, they were under the wrath and curse of God, I marvel, Melville, they did not stone us!"[7]

Here I must tell Wesley's story of his conversion at

Aldersgate, May 24, 1738. I've waited until now to do so because the core of that conversion was the gift of assurance. Recall the bare outline of Wesley's life:

Wesley was a priest in the Church of England, a very religious person who, from earliest childhood, had been taught the doctrines of the church. His mother, Susanna, was an exceptional person. She had nineteen children, and all of the children who survived were given two hours of religious instruction by their mother each week. What a task, and what a commitment on the part of a mother!

Having been nurtured by his mother and by his father, Samuel, who was also a priest in the Church of England, John Wesley had a conversion experience in 1725 while a student at Oxford University. (We'll come back to that conversion later because it played a significant role in Wesley's life.) There are few examples in history of a more disciplined religious person. He rose at four in the morning to pray and study; he met with others who had joined him in what was called the Holy Club; he visited prisons; he gave all his money to the poor except what was absolutely necessary for his own living. He was almost neurotically preoccupied with the right use of his time.

He was a man desperately seeking salvation and an assurance of his salvation. He was tirelessly bent upon achieving that, and as a merciless taskmaster, he drove himself in all the religious disciplines and services that could be imagined. He even came to America as a missionary to the Indians—serving for a time in southern Georgia near Savannah. But all of that was a failure; and it seemed to Wesley that his whole life was doomed to failure.

On the ship bound for America, Wesley came in touch with some Moravians, and they influenced his life tremendously. A storm battered the ship to the point that even veteran seamen panicked. Everyone was terrified except the Moravians. They were calm and assured. They gathered together, prayed, and sang hymns, apparently oblivious to the storm. Wesley saw in them the peace that he desperately longed for, and he learned that they called that inner peace "assurance."

In Georgia, he met a Moravian pastor, August Spangenburg, who made a tremendous impression on him. At their meeting, Spangenburg instantly pressed the question, "Have you the witness of the Spirit within yourself? Does the Spirit of God bear witness with your spirit that you are a child of God?" Wesley was surprised and did not know what to answer.

Spangenburg then asked, "Do you know Jesus Christ?" After a pause, Wesley responded, "I know that He is the Savior of the world." "True," Spangenburg said, "but do you know that He has saved you?"

Wesley's reply was, "I hope He has died to save me," to which Spangenburg pressed, "Do you know yourself?"

Wesley responded, "I do," but later wrote in his *Journal,* "I fear they were vain words." He knew he didn't have what the Moravians had—assurance, the witness of the Spirit. He went home from Georgia downcast in mind, despondent in spirit, pierced in his heart with the futility of all his efforts and the emptiness of his soul.

After a short time back in England, he visited his brother Charles, who was sick in bed with pleurisy. Charles confided to John that in the crisis of the illness, when his life was in peril, he had experienced the assurance of God's love and felt that no matter what happened, everything was going to be all right. Charles was able to accept each day as a gift from God and enjoy it.

John continued to struggle. He had labored as diligently as Charles had. He had worked for that assurance of God's love probably harder than anyone in all of England. And you can imagine that when he saw that Charles had received what he himself had so struggled for, he was profoundly discouraged.

It was in that despondent mood he went to a prayer meeting on Aldersgate Street in London on May 24, 1738. A layperson read Luther's preface to the Epistle to the Romans, and something new happened in John Wesley's life: "I felt my heart strangely warmed. I felt I did trust in Christ, Christ alone, for my salvation; and an assurance was given me that he had taken away *my* sins, even *mine*, and saved *me* from the law of sin and death."[8]

A friend, Mark Trotter, has imaginatively suggested that the experience of John and Charles Wesley, coupled with the memory of the Moravians' response to the storm at sea, was the inspiration for the first verse of Charles's hymn, "Jesus, Lover of My Soul":

> *Jesus, lover of my soul,*
> *Let me to thy bosom fly,*
> *While the nearer waters roll,*
> *While the tempest still is high:*
> *Hide me, O my Savior, hide,*
> *Till the storm of life is past;*
> *Safe into the haven guide;*
> *O receive my soul at last!*[9]

THE GIFT OF ASSURANCE

Aldersgate was the watershed. It transformed Wesley from a slave to a son. He *knew* he was a Christian. That's a key word: He *knew* that, in his words, "Christ had taken away *my* sins, even *mine*, and saved *me* from the law of sin and death." In Paul's words, he did not receive the spirit of slavery to fall back into fear, but the spirit of sonship—the sonship that enables us to cry, "Abba! Father!"

Aldersgate was an evangelical conversion that resulted in assurance. In his book, *John Wesley: His Life and Theology*, Robert Tuttle has captured the essence of Wesley's witness about this experience. Writing in the first person for Wesley, he has him say:

> To summarize, Aldersgate was indeed a watershed between law and grace. The experience of faith, love, and power, as well as assurance, is no small thing, but the sum total of my agonizing search for the life of God in the soul of man must be considered. Struggle alone never justified a man; but man is rarely justified without it. Man

71

can never be saved by works; but he can never be saved without them either. I was determined not to substitute one extreme for the other. A measure of faith had left me blind to my own dependence upon self-righteousness. I was not to be saved *by* works but *for* works. The Aldersgate experience taught me that faith alone was the source of power. The experience of these last fifty years has proven this to be true without doubt.

Following Aldersgate I then had to pursue God as wholeheartedly by grace through faith as I had previously done by the law. I was a "brand plucked from the burning" and the intensity of my desire to serve God (since 1725) perhaps made Aldersgate inevitable.

"Unless the servants of God halt the way, they will receive the adoption of sons. They will receive the *faith* of the children of God, by His *revealing* His only begotten Son in their hearts." Yet, I had to keep moving. Faith is a process. Had I stopped there the experience of Aldersgate would not have lasted through the night.

So, the Aldersgate experience was the difference not between saving faith and condemnation, the almost and the altogether Christian, but between servant and son.[10]

Now once the Spirit makes that witness to us, the witness of assurance is continually verified. It is verified in at least four ways:

1. We know that we've repented of our sins and will continue to repent daily.

2. We are aware of change in our lives, and the awareness of assurance grows within us if we see changes continually happening.

3. Assurance is ours if we are aware of a new character being produced in us, if the fruits of the Spirit are growing in our lives

4. We know assurance if we find joy in the service of God.

Few experiences could provide more power in our lives than to have assurance of our salvation. Think what it could do for us:

Our timidity and uncertainty about witnessing would be dissolved. We would not be intimidated by those "buttonhole witnesses" who come on like gangbusters. We would know that attitudes of tenderness, patience, and understanding, as well as words, are authentic testimonies.

We would not get overwrought with our Christian friends who insist on future security, for we would be assured of our present relationship with Christ.

We would be joyous in our service for God, but not driven in our works or mistaken in the notion that our works would save us.

We would be delivered from frantic preoccupation with taking our spiritual temperature minute by minute, because we could relax in our trust of the Lord.

And all of that would help us, wouldn't it? It certainly helped Wesley. On Thursday morning, May 25, the day after his conversion, he wrote,

> The moment I awaked, "Jesus Master," was in my heart and in my mouth; and I found all my strength lay in keeping my eyes fixed upon him, and my soul waiting on him continually. Then at St. Paul's in the afternoon, I could taste the good word of God in the anthem which began, "My song shall be always of the loving kindness of the Lord: with my mouth will I ever be showing forth thy truth from one generation to another." Yet the enemy injected a fear, "If thou dost believe, why is there not a more sensible change?" I answered "That I know not. But this I know, I have now peace with God." And I sin not today, and Jesus my master has forbid me to take no thought for the morrow.
>
> "But is not any sort of fear," continued the tempter, "a proof that thou dost not believe?" I desired my master to answer for me, and opened his book upon those words of St. Paul, "Without were fightings, within

were fears." Then, inferred I, well may fears be within me; but I must go on, and tread them under my feet.[11]

That can be our experience, with the assurance given us that we are no longer slaves but children—and that we've not been given the spirit of fear, but the spirit of adoption, whereby we cry, "Abba! Father!" We can keep singing the hymn that Charles wrote in celebration of his and his brother's conversion:

> *Where shall my wondering soul begin?*
> *How shall I all to heaven aspire?*
> *A slave redeemed from death and sin,*
> *A brand plucked from eternal fire,*
> *How shall I equal triumphs raise,*
> *Or sing my great deliverer's praise?*[12]

I ask you to meet two challenges to keep your assurance alive: This day, and every day, rejoice in the salvation that is yours. This day, and every day, repent of every sin and renew your faith commitment to Jesus Christ. And the Holy Spirit of peace "will keep your hearts and your minds in Christ Jesus" (Phil. 4:7).

6
The Church:
The Dwelling Place
of Wonder

For this reason, because I have heard of your faith in the
Lord Jesus and your love toward all the saints, I do not
cease to give thanks for you, remembering you in my
prayers, that the God of our Lord Jesus Christ, the
Father of glory, may give you a spirit of wisdom and of
revelation in the knowledge of him, having the eyes of
your hearts enlightened, that you may know what is the
hope to which he has called you, what are the riches of
his glorious inheritance in the saints, and what is the
immeasurable greatness of his power in us who believe,
according to the working of his great might which he
accomplished in Christ when he raised him from the dead
and made him sit at his right hand in the heavenly places,
far above all rule and authority and power and dominion,
and above every name that is named, not only in this age
but also in that which is to come; and he has put all things
under his feet and has made him the head over all things
for the church, which is his body, the fulness of him who
fills all in all (Eph. 1:15–23).

Somewhere along the way (I think I got it from one of my
heroes, Bishop Gerald Kennedy), I connected a drama critic's
definition of the theater with an understanding of the church.
"The theater," said the critic, "is the dwelling place of
wonder." Isn't that marvelous? But it's really a better
definition of the church than it is of the theater. Think about it.

THE DWELLING PLACE OF THE GOSPEL

Consider first that the church is *the dwelling place of wonder of the gospel.*Wesley defined the visible church as a congregation of faithful people, "in which the pure Word of God is preached." For Wesley, "the Scriptures are a complete rule of faith and practice; and they are clear in all necessary points."[1]

In his pamphlet "The Character of a Methodist," Wesley said: "As to all opinions which do not strike at the root of Christianity, we think and let think. So that whatsoever they are, whether right or wrong, there are no distinguishing marks of a Methodist."[2]

One of the distinguishing characteristics of Wesleyanism throughout its history is that it has been catholic (that is, inclusive) in its spirit. The United Methodist Church has been ecumenical and open to other denominations. For example, we do not require rebaptism when persons from other Christian churches present themselves for membership. (We will explore this more fully in chapter 8.)

This does not mean that we are unconcerned about doctrine and theology. When people make a profession of faith and desire to be baptized, we ask these questions:

- Do you truly and earnestly repent of your sins and accept Jesus Christ as your Savior?

- Do you believe in God, the Father Almighty, maker of heaven and earth; and in Jesus Christ His only Son our Lord; and in the Holy Spirit, the Lord, the giver of life?

- Do you desire to be baptized in this faith?

- Will you then obediently keep God's holy will and commandments and walk in the same all the days of your life?

When people who have been baptized come to be confirmed in the church, we ask similar questions:

- Do you here, in the presence of God, and of this congregation, renew the solemn promise and vow that you made, or that was made in your name, at your baptism?

- Do you confess Jesus Christ as your Lord and Savior and pledge your allegiance to His kingdom?

- Do you receive and profess the Christian faith as contained in the Scriptures of the Old and New Testaments?

- Do you promise according to the grace given you to live a Christian life and always remain a faithful member of Christ's holy church?

We assume that a positive response to these questions is essential as a Christian affirmation of faith and for membership in the church. The church is the dwelling place of the wonder of the gospel, where the faith once delivered to the saints—the faith that has come to us primarily through Scripture—is proclaimed, responded to, and lived out in the world.

Ephesians 4:1–6 was a controlling text for Wesley's understanding of the church. In these verses the unity of believers is emphasized, under the classic affirmation of our unity in "one Lord, one faith, one baptism" (Eph. 4:5). When Wesley talked about "one faith," he did not mean a single code of doctrine. He confessed his indebtedness to Roman Catholic, Lutheran, Reformed, Puritan, and Anglican traditions. "Right doctrine" was never a condition for membership in the Methodist society, but "a desire to flee from the wrath to come."

Even so, Wesley was not ambiguous about the "one faith" of the church. He tenaciously believed that the fundamental doctrines of Christianity were set forth in Scripture. These doctrines had been articulated in the major creeds of the first 450 years of church history and were described in the Thirty-nine Articles of the Anglican church.

77

Wesley singled out three things that are essential to a visible church:

> First: Living faith, without which, indeed, there can be no church at all, neither visible or invisible. Secondly: Preaching, and consequently hearing, the pure word of God, else that faith would languish and die. And, thirdly, a due administration of the Sacraments—the ordinary means whereby God increaseth faith.[3]

When we say that the church is the dwelling place of the gospel, we mean that Scripture is preeminent as the rule of faith and action, and that the real question of faith is not so much content but, How does faith operate in the church? Thus we come to the following affirmation of the church:

THE DWELLING PLACE OF CHRISTIAN FELLOWSHIP

The church is *the dwelling place of Christian fellowship*. Wesley had an exceedingly strong doctrine of the church. His commitment to the church was unquestioned. He remained a priest in the Church of England, he resisted the idea of the Methodist movement becoming a church, and he urged all the members of Methodist societies to stay in communion with and receive the sacraments of the Anglican church—all this and his total life demonstrated his love and commitment to the established church.

Yet Wesley knew that it took more than hearing the Word and participating in the sacraments for Christian growth and discipleship. A deep fellowship for mutual encouragement, examination, accountability, and service was essential. Wesley talked about one loving heart setting another heart on fire. And that's a powerful image.

The fellowship for hearts setting each other on fire in the early Wesleyan movement was the class meeting. This was Wesley's effort to restore the depth and transforming power of the fellowship present in the early church. He felt that the Church of England did not sufficiently provide for the fellowship of Christian people, which he sensed to have been the unique characteristic of the early church. Speaking of the failure of the fellowship in the Church of England, he wrote,

> Look east or west, north or south; name what parish you please: Is this Christian fellowship there? Rather, are not the bulk of parishioners a mere rope of sand? What Christian connection is there between them? What intercourse in spiritual things? What watching over each other's souls? What bearing of one another's burdens?[4]

So Wesley established class meetings to provide the fellowship of one loving heart setting another on fire. The class meetings were neither rivals to nor substitutes for the church in its ministry. They complemented the church by offering a more intense and personal encounter of faith and grace within a context of mutual accountability. The class meeting conserved the results of revival preaching and became the principal avenue of pastoral care during the Wesleyan revival. In the class meeting five questions were asked:

1. What known sins have you committed since our last meeting?

2. What temptations have you met with?

3. How were you delivered?

4. What have you thought, said, or done, of which you doubt whether it be sin or not?

5. Have you nothing you desire to keep secret?[5]

That's a rather tough agenda, isn't it? Most of us would resist it. But it worked. It started a fire burning in the hearts of people which set other hearts on fire. In fact, it started a revival fire in England and in America. It may well be that the precise agenda is not appropriate for us—though it may be. What is not only appropriate, but absolutely essential, is that the church provide the setting of fellowship where people care

79

for and minister to one another. That's the fellowship in which one loving heart sets another on fire, and the church is to be the dwelling place of the wonder of Christian fellowship.

This is how Aristides described the Christians to the Roman emperor Hadrian:

> They love one another. They never fail to help widows; they save orphans from those who would hurt them. If they have something they give freely to the man who has nothing; if they see a stranger, they take him home, and are happy, as though he were a real brother. They don't consider themselves brothers in the usual sense, but brothers instead through the spirit, in God.[6]

THE DWELLING PLACE OF CHRIST

The church is *the dwelling place of Christ*. That's a bold word, but the church is a bold dream of God. Go back to the Scripture with which we began this chapter. When Jesus was raised from the dead, God

> made him sit at his right hand in the heavenly places, far above all rule and authority and power and dominion, and above every name that is named, not only in this age but also in that which is to come; and he has put all things under his feet and has made him the head over all things for the church, which is his body, the fulness of him who fills all in all (Eph. 1:20–23).

In this particular passage, Paul tried to communicate the breadth of Christ's power. It is resurrection power—the power God "accomplished in Christ when he raised him from the dead" (v. 20).

It is ascension power—"and made him sit at his right hand in the heavenly places" (v. 20). It is dominion power— "far above all rule and authority and power and domin- ion, . . . and he has put all things under his feet and has made him the head over all things for the church" (vv. 21–22). In these three phrases Paul poured out his surging soul as he

80

sought to do the impossible—to capture in words the immeasurable power and glory of God's work in Christ: resurrection, ascension, and dominion.

Ephesians has been called the "Epistle of the Ascension," and that it is because in it we meet the exalted power of Christ. In the modern church, we make too little of the Ascension of Christ. How much thought do you give it? Does the Ascension have an impact on your life? The early Christians were post-Resurrection, post-Ascension Christians. They knew the gospel story: a Jesus who was once a baby in His mother's arms—but not that now; a Jesus who was a carpenter, teacher, companion, and friend—but not that now; One whose healing love mercifully blessed all He touched, all He could see and hear and speak to—but He is not limited by time and space now; a self-giving Suffering Servant who hung on a cross, pouring out His life and love on our behalf—but He is not hanging there now. God raised Him from the dead!

But there is more: This Jesus ascended, and the curtain went up on a new act in the drama. Pentecost has happened. The Spirit of this ascended One was poured out on His followers, and the church was born. The ascended One is "far above all rule and authority and power and dominion." His name is exalted "above every name that is named, not only in this age but also in that which is to come." Everything has been put under His feet. He is the head, the authority. He has been given dominion. And the church is His body—the fullness of Him who fills all in all.

81

Do you stir with excitement as I do when you think of that? The church is the dwelling place of the wonder of Christ. We—the church—are His body!

For Wesley, the lordship of Christ was the Christian's greatest joy. Living under Christ's lordship provides the experience that Wesley described as "sitting in heavenly places with Christ." But this is to be no passive stance, no resting calmly in rapture and ease. Christ's lordship calls for disciplined obedience and attending upon the means of grace that we will discuss in chapter 9. Wesley called the church "a body of people united in the service of God."

What does it mean for us to be the body of Christ? I can never forget how the late Bishop Kenneth W. Copeland answered this question. He said that to be Christ to the world means that *we must see through the eyes of Christ*. And what does it mean to see through the eyes of Christ? Through Christ's eyes, there is no East or West, no black or white, no slave or free, no male or female. All are one in Christ.

Through Christ's eyes, every person is of worth, and the church must respond in loving concern for all persons. We must not be selective in our outreach, seeking only those who are like us. In Christ's eyes, every person is a person for whom Christ died.

Not only must we see through Christ's eyes, but *we must speak with the voice of Christ*. Do you remember what Jesus said when, on the Sabbath day, He stood in the Nazareth synagogue and launched His public ministry? He read from Isaiah: "The Spirit of the Lord is upon me, because he has anointed me to preach good news to the poor. He has sent me to proclaim release to the captives and recovering of sight to the blind, to set at liberty those who are oppressed, to proclaim the acceptable year of the Lord" (Luke 4:18–19). If the church is going to be the body of Christ, we must have the voice of Christ.

And as the voice of Christ, we must fulfill in our world today this ancient prophecy that Jesus declared was fulfilled in him. We must speak with the voice of Christ to humankind in every situation and every condition. It's not a matter of a social gospel or a personal gospel. It's a matter of the Good News of Jesus Christ. War and peace, inflation and the national deficit, how the government spends the taxes we pay, where and how people live, abortion, pornography, ethnic relationships—whatever is of concern to human beings is a concern of the gospel. The gospel has something to say for our human plight, whether that plight involves our politics or our economics. The gospel can't be forbidden from going into any area of human life. No area is off-limits to Christ. The church must speak fearlessly and compassionately the words of God's Good News to every person, wherever that person is.

Not only must the church see through the eyes of Christ and speak through the voice of Christ, but the church must *heal with the hands of Christ*. The ministry of the church is the ministry of redemption and healing.

In his book, *Immortal Tidings in Mortal Hands,* Bishop Arthur J. Moore tells how the Old Testament phrase, the "excellency of Carmel" (Isa. 35:2 KJV) came to have deep religious meaning for him. At first it really meant nothing beyond its poetic grace. Then he happened to hear a famous archeologist lecture on the subject of Mount Carmel. The archeologist said that on this bald mountain, lovely flowers were found. There was no known explanation for their beauty among the blistered rocks. This was the "excellency of Carmel" for Bishop Moore, and so the good bishop drew this conclusion: "Then I began to understand something of the rich suggestiveness of this saying. Jesus came to give beauty for ashes, joy for mourning; to make an old world young again, and to work his ancient miracle of renewal and release in the lives of those who were helpless."

The church as Christ's body continues this work of redemption and healing among the poor and the elderly; in the divisions that continue between races, rich and poor, male and female; among those who are economically deprived and politically oppressed; among those who have everything except what they need to make what they have worthwhile and meaningful; and with the emotionally and mentally ravaged, those in the tenacious grip of alcohol and other drugs.

Finally, the church *breathes with Christ's Spirit*. You see, we're not only a human organization, we're also a spiritual organism. Our life is the life of Christ's Spirit. His Spirit gives us power. Here is a vivid example of that power in action:

83

A young Christian, a singer, was imprisoned with thousands of others in the National Stadium in Santiago. As he stood among the frightened and demoralized prisoners, he began a solitary song in praise of his Lord. A guitar was passed to him and the Spirit began to blow. Soon thousands were singing with him. As usual, the authorities were threatened by the power of God's Spirit moving so freely and openly. So they seized the young man and took him away. When he returned, not only had his guitar been smashed, but he had no fingers. Horrified, his fellow prisoners drew back, but he walked into the empty space between them, lifted his bloody hands, and again began to sing with a glory on his face. Once more the Spirit began to move, the people took up the song, and predictably the guards moved in again. This time when he came back, he had no tongue. Many wept as they realized what had been done to him. Everyone was watching. For awhile he stood motionless. Some thought he was fainting. But then they realized that his graceful, silent swing was a dance. And soon they were all swaying silently with him, inspired by his glory, moved by his spirit. This time when the guards came, they thought they would end it all, and they shot him dead. But the Spirit continued to blow.[7]

The Spirit blows today in the dynamic renewal of the church in Korea; in the courageous stand of the church against apartheid in South Africa; in the luminous life of Christians in Central and South America, in their witness on behalf of the poor; and in our local communities of faith that continue to win people for Christ, serve others in His name, and preach the gospel with clarity and conviction.

The Spirit continues to blow through the church that is Christ's body. And as the Spirit blows, the gates of hell cannot prevail against this church.

Does that make your heart happy? Do you feel the jubilant joy of it? Do you feel the pulsating power of it? We are the church. We belong to the body of Christ. And as His body, we are the dwelling place of wonder!

7
Holiness of Heart and Life

But if you call yourself a Jew and rely upon the law and boast of your relation to God and know his will and approve what is excellent, because you are instructed in the law, and if you are sure that you are a guide to the blind, a light to those who are in darkness, a corrector of the foolish, a teacher of children, having in the law the embodiment of knowledge and truth—you then who teach others, will you not teach yourself? While you preach against stealing, do you steal? You who say that one must not commit adultery, do you commit adultery? You who abhor idols, do you rob temples? You who boast in the law, do you dishonor God by breaking the law? For, as it is written, "The name of God is blasphemed among the Gentiles because of you." . . . He is not a real Jew who is one outwardly, nor is true circumcision something external and physical. He is a Jew who is one inwardly, and real circumcision is a matter of the heart, spiritual and not literal. His praise is not from men but from God (Rom. 2:17–24, 28–29).

A Stanford University psychologist recently set forth a theory called "cognitive dissonance." It refers to a person's awareness of the big gap between ideals and actions, between what one believes and what one does, between an individual's goals and deeds.

We all have that problem. Paul felt the Jews faced the problem in a special way, though they didn't know it. Do you know any people in history who have clung more tenaciously to a name than the Jews—a name rich in ethnic, social, and religious connotations? I doubt if there is a name more pronounced in history and in present-day culture in designating a particular people than the word *Jew*.

Circumcision was the identifying mark for the Jew. Paul challenged his fellow Jews and the meaning of circumcision, calling for a "circumcision" of the heart. Paul affirmed the call of the Jews to be "God's own people." God had made a covenant with them to be a chosen race. To them the law had been given. The Jews were proud of that; therein was a problem. In their pride, they became the victims of cognitive dissonance. Paul didn't use that phrase because he was a student of Gamaliel, not of the psychology department at Stanford University. But he did address this cognitive dissonance" of the Jews when he accused them of failing to harmonize identity and action, belief and practice.

CIRCUMCISION OF THE HEART

The core concept of this Scripture passage from Romans 2 is "circumcision," and that is the image upon which we build this chapter—Paul's call for a "circumcision" of the heart.

The problem was that many Jews had allowed circumcision, that unique mark of identification as a covenant people, to become superficial and meaningless. "Circumcision indeed is of value if you obey the law; but if you break the law, your circumcision becomes uncircumcision" (Rom. 2:25).

Paul made his case more clearly: "For he is not a real Jew who is one outwardly, nor is true circumcision something external and physical. He is a Jew who is one inwardly, and real circumcision is a matter of the heart, spiritual and not literal. His praise is not from men but from God" (Rom. 28–29).

John Wesley used the verse, "Real circumcision is a

matter of the heart, spiritual and not literal," as the text for his sermon, "Circumcision of the Heart," preached at Oxford University on January 1, 1733. This is the only sermon Wesley preached before his conversion at Aldersgate in 1738 that he kept in its original form and used throughout his life in teaching Methodists. This consistency underscores a distinctively Wesleyan view of the Christian way: holiness of heart and life, or personal and social holiness.

As mentioned in the last chapter, in 1725 Wesley had a conversion to the ideal of holy living. He never abandoned that ideal, though it was cast in a different framework after his Aldersgate conversion.

Between 1725 and his Aldersgate experience in 1738, he consistently misplaced holiness. He was driven by the idea that one must be holy in order to be justified. That was the futile process that drove Wesley to the deep despondency that eventually brought him to Aldersgate. One of the decisive shifts that came in his conversion at Aldersgate was a reversal of the order of salvation—justification preceded holiness, not vice versa.

There is a story, perhaps apocryphal, of Bishop J. Lloyd Decell's calling in a pastor who had been disappointed in his appointment. The bishop said, "My brother, I want you to know that this appointment has been sanctified by long hours of thought and prayer."

The man replied, "Bishop, that's the strangest Methodist theology I ever heard."

The bishop asked, "What do you mean?"

The fellow answered, "According to Methodist theology, a thing has to be justified before it can be sanctified."[1]

The man was right—though his argument has nothing to do with how bishops make appointments, I'm sure. Justification precedes sanctification. Yet, Wesleyans, according to Wesley, "maintain with equal zeal and diligence, the doctrine of free, full, present justification, on the one hand, and of entire sanctification both of heart and life, on the other; being as tenacious of inward holiness as any Mystic, and of outward, as any Pharisee."[2]

87

A part of Wesley's genius was his ability to adapt and combine diverse elements into a synthesis, to bring harmony out of what on the surface was disparate. Howard Snyder clearly points this out:

> The Bible says salvation is all of grace, not of works. It also says we are able to work out our salvation, that faith without works is dead. Wesley's way out of this paradox was through Galatians 5:6—"faith working by love." This became a favorite passage and theme. True faith shed God's love abroad in the heart, which became the fountainhead of "all inward and outward holiness."
>
> Wesley's genius, under God, lay in developing and maintaining a synthesis in doctrine and practice that kept biblical paradoxes paired and powerful. He held together faith and works, doctrine and experience, the individual and the social, the concerns of time and eternity[3]

So the synthesis of personal and social holiness, holiness of heart and life, has always been a central theme of the Wesleyan message.

THE LOVE OF GOD AND NEIGHBOR

It is important to keep a perspective on at least a skeletal outline of Wesley's thought, especially about our need of salvation. Again, Snyder states it clearly:

> Wesley's starting point was not the decrees of God nor the logic required to solve theological paradoxes. Rather it was what Scripture affirms: God is sovereign; beside him there is no other god; all salvation depends on his initiative and working. But humans, even though sinful, still have a measure of freedom. And if they turn to God, they can be his co-workers in the concerns of the Kingdom.
>
> . . . In a passage typical of many others, Wesley says that true Christianity is "the love of God in our neighbour; the image of God stamped on the heart; the life of God in the soul of man; the mind that was in Christ, enabling us to walk as Christ also walked."[4]

For Wesley, it was a matter of the circumcision of the heart that issued in love of God and love of neighbor—holiness of heart and life.

It was captured clearly and succinctly at the formal establishment of Methodism in America at the 1784 Christmas Conference in Baltimore. The question was asked, "What can we rightly expect to be the task of Methodists in America?" The answer came clear and strong: "To reform a continent and spread scriptural holiness across the land." That's personal and social holiness.

But what does all this mean? Simply put, it means that we as Christians are to be holy as God is holy, that the church is to be that demonstration plot of holiness set down in an unholy world. Jesus said it means that we are to love God with all our heart, mind, soul, and strength, and our neighbor as ourselves. And Paul said it means that faith without works is dead, and *the work of faith is love.*

Mother Theresa of Calcutta is a luminous example of one who took God's call to holiness seriously. She said, "Our progress in holiness depends on God and ourselves—on God's grace and on our will to be holy."[5]

And another modern person who took God's holiness seriously was Dag Hammarskjöld, who said, "The road to holiness necessarily passes through the world of action."[6]

Wesley would affirm this commitment: "This is the sum of Christian perfection—loving God, and loving our neighbor—these contain the whole of Christian perfection!"[7]

Wesley spoke of "inward holiness," that is, love of God and the assurance of God's love for us. And he spoke of "outward holiness," that is, love of neighbor and deeds of kindness. He was fond of speaking of persons being "happy and holy." For him the two experiences were not opposites, but actually one reality. "Why are not you happy?" Wesley frequently asked. Then he would answer, "Other circumstances may concur, but the main reason is because you are not holy."[8]

But never was it personal alone. In his extravagant way

of stating things, he made clear the unity of faith and action. "Christianity is essentially a social religion," Wesley declared, "and to turn it into a solitary religion is indeed to destroy it."[9]

What I'd like us to do now is simply underscore the two separately—personal holiness and social holiness—and then speak briefly about the church as the holy people who will be the primary witnesses of holiness of heart and life.

PERSONAL HOLINESS

First, let's look at personal holiness. Perhaps the clearest scriptural call to personal holiness is Romans 12:1–2: "I appeal to you therefore, brethren, by the mercies of God, to present your bodies as a living sacrifice, holy and acceptable to God, which is your spiritual worship. Do not be conformed to this world but be transformed by the renewal of your mind, that you may prove what is the will of God, what is good and acceptable and perfect."

In the chapter on sanctification, I quoted from 1 Thessalonians 4:3, 7: "For this is the will of God, your sanctification. . . . For God has not called us for uncleanness, but 90 in holiness." In talking about holiness to the Thessalonians, Paul spoke of their relationship with others: "Do not transgress or wrong your brothers," he said (1 Thess. 4:6, para.). That was a negative expression, but the positive, simple admonition is: "Love one another."

Do we do our jobs in holiness? But more than that, do we live our whole lives loving one another? That's the key to personal holiness.

Chuck Colson has written an illuminating and challenging book entitled *Loving God*. It is primarily a book on personal and social holiness. In one chapter, "The Everyday Business of Holiness," he makes the case that holiness is loving and obeying God. He gives a series of personal vignettes that illustrate some telling truths about holiness. Here are those truths:

1. Holiness is obeying God—loving one another as God loved us.

2. Holiness is obeying God—even when it is against our own interests.

3. Holiness is obeying God—sharing God's love, even when it is inconvenient.

4. Holiness is obeying God—finding ways to help those in need.

That's a good witness in our own quest for holiness.

SOCIAL HOLINESS

Now, let's consider specifically the wider arena of *social holiness*.

Wesley said, "The gospel of Christ knows no religion but social; no holiness but social." The social impact of the Wesleyan revival, though sometimes exaggerated, is hardly measurable. Marquis W. Childs and Douglas Cater conclude that "out of the light kindled by Wesley and the evangelical revival came the great drive for reform movements that had a direct and continuing relationship to the life of the past 100 years."[10] Kenneth E. Boulding asserted, "It was not the economists who liberated the slaves or who passed the Factory Acts, but the rash and ignorant Christians."[11]

Wesley was at the heart of it. One of the last letters he wrote was to William Wilberforce, blessing him and urging him on in his antislavery fight in England. "Go on," he said, "in the name of God and in the power of his might, till even American slavery (the vilest that ever saw the sun) shall vanish away before it."[12]

Wesley and the early Wesleyan movement addressed several areas of social concern: poverty, slavery, prisons, liquor, war, and education. It is not a matter of recent concern that Wesleyans have a social creed that speaks to these same issues as well as others.

Our temptation when we consider social holiness is to address the obvious—issues such as pornography, abortion, and homosexuality. In our zealous reaction to these, we disregard other issues that are equally serious, though perhaps more subtle.

We spend a great deal of our righteous indignation and energy over issues such as prayer in public schools. Let me share a personal witness. I spent ten years of my life at The Upper Room in a ministry focused on prayer. I'm committed to prayer. Yet, the issue of prayer in public schools is not as simple as many of our politicians—who want the votes of us Evangelical Christians—would make it.

I am committed to prayer, but there is a difference between Christian prayer and other forms of prayer. When we lived in southern California, I would have had real reservations about my children being led in prayer by the young teacher who had just come back from her latest weekend with a popular Eastern guru from Tibet. Or by the teacher (deeply religious, but not Christian) who had just finished a crash course on "How to Conduct a Seance," which he thought prayer was all about.

Do you see the point I'm making? I do not want persons who are not Christian—some who may be explicitly non-Christian—modeling prayer for my children. I want to give other persons the right to guide the religious training of their children, also.

Christian prayer is an act of the people of God who are committed to God's sovereignty and holiness and to the saving grace of Jesus Christ. Any other prayer is what the prophets referred to as the "noise of solemn assemblies" (Amos 5:21), and what Jesus referred to as "praying with ourselves" (see Luke 18:11). The responsibility for teaching Christian prayer belongs not to the public schools but to the family and to the church.

Consider another example of our tendency to restrict our holy and righteous outrage against the obvious. The United Methodist Church is clear in its position on homosexuality.

92

Within our Social Principles we read: "We insist that all persons are entitled to have their human and civil rights insured, though we do not condone the practice of homosexuality and consider this practice incompatible with Christian teaching." That being clear, let me make my point without anyone mistaking my position and the official position of the United Methodist Church:

The Scripture that people use most in the condemnation of homosexuality is the story of Sodom and Gomorrah. The usual reason given for the destruction of these cities was sexual immorality—and that certainly was one reason for it. Yet, when the prophet Ezekiel talked about it, he said: "This was the guilt of your sister Sodom: she and her daughters had pride, surfeit of food, and prosperous ease, but did not aid the poor and needy" (Ezek. 16:49).

The point is clear: In our passion to scrub America clean, we often narrow the scope of Christian concern. When we crusade on a few particular issues, we implicitly embrace those things not on our hit list or the hit list of our favorite politician; thus, we align ourselves with the subtle sins of privilege, power, civil religion, and idolatrous nationalism.

Certainly, social holiness has to do with pornography, abortion, and homosexuality—but it also has to do with people's becoming calloused in "prosperous ease," taking no thought of aiding the poor and needy.

We're rightly upset about the present economic situation of our nation—the staggering deficit that grows daily. I hope we are learning that there are limits to what we once thought was the endless abundance of the American economy. Government deficits must be curbed, lest they continue to fuel inflation, which is morally indefensible and threatens the very fabric of our national life.

But let's keep perspective. If inflation is a moral issue, as we believe it to be, so too is society's concern (or unconcern) for the poor, the disadvantaged, and the oppressed. We Christians know from the Old Testament prophets that almighty God has a fearsome judgment of a people who would "sell . . . the needy for a pair of shoes" (Amos 2:6). And we know from Jesus himself that our judgment will be based on how we respond to the "least of these" (Matt. 25:40).

We could spend pages discussing further questions about social holiness:

- What does social holiness have to do with a morally decadent society that no longer questions premarital and extramarital sex; that has trivialized marriage and brought about a cultural situation in which there are almost as many divorces as there are first-time marriages each year?

- What does social holiness have to do with a prison system that contributes to making a criminal society rather than preventing crime and reforming offenders?

- What does social holiness have to do with a nuclear arms race that clouds the world with ominous fear and drains the financial resources of the major superpowers?

- What does social holiness have to do with housing patterns that have resegregated the public school system?

I can't answer these questions with a specific plan of action. But I believe the questions themselves call us to a commitment to holiness of heart and life. I ask these baffling questions to show that their answers must be preceded by something far more crucial. That's what I want to address now.

IN THE MEANTIME . . .

What can we rightly expect to be the task of Wesleyans in America? To reform a continent and spread scriptural holiness across the land. What is required for such a mission? The circumcision of the heart that will identify us as those people who love and seek to obey God, and who are committed to the promise that the kingdom of this world will one day become the kingdom of Christ.

But in the meantime—ah, that's the point!—in the meantime, what is to be our task?

Our first and primary task is to be faithful to Christ. We are called to be the church, to be the kind of community we need to be in order to be faithful to the Christian gospel—to be the church we talked about in the last chapter, *seeing* through the eyes of Christ, *speaking* with the voice of Christ, *healing* with the hands of Christ, and *breathing* with the Spirit of Christ.

Our first task, then, is not a political or social one, though it will certainly make an impact politically and socially. We are to be the church—to keep criticizing our message, ministry, and life together so that we become who God calls us to be, a people formed by the gospel.

William H. Willimon has put the case in a puzzling way: "We best criticize the world by being the church." Then he builds his case:

> Our aim is not effectiveness, but a prophetic demonstration that Jesus makes possible a new social order based not upon what works or competing self-interest, but upon his Lordship.

> This is not a withdrawal from the world. It is a plea to confront the world on our own terms. The imperatives, "Come unto me," and "Do this in remembrance of me," theologically precede, "Go ye unto all the world."

> In its very existence, the church serves the world, not by running errands, but by providing a light, that is, providing an imaginative alternative for society. The gospel call is an invitation to be a part of a people who are struggling to create those structures which the world can never achieve through governmental power and balanced self-interest. By its very existence the church is a paradigm for a society, a demonstration which the world considers impossible.[13]

95

This does not mean that we do not labor diligently as Christians for justice and peace. It does not mean that we do not take seriously the political process and work for changed systems and structures, for legislation and political leaders who will serve the common good. But it does mean that we will not put our hope in these. We do not place our trust in any political party or persons, any economic or governmental promise of panacea.

We perfect our lives in holiness. We live together in the church as a people who have already tasted the kingdom. We demonstrate by who we are, what we say, and how we live that there is a kingdom reality that transcends all earthly systems and programs.

> *O living Church, thine errand speed;*
> *Fulfill thy task sublime;*
> *With bread of life earth's hungers feed;*
> *Redeem the evil time!*[14]

Jim Harnish, a preacher friend in Florida, shared a story about the power of a photograph, a story that says something about what the church should be. Yousaf Karsh was the photographer. Perhaps you know his works. He is a Canadian photographer who has spent the past fifty years taking photographic portraits of the world's great people.

The only portrait Karsh ever took of a person's back was of Pablo Casals in a small French abbey in 1954. Karsh writes that as he was setting up his equipment, Casals began playing Bach on his cello. Karsh was so enthralled by the music that he says he almost forgot why he was there. He took his portrait of Casals with the little bald-headed man bent over his cello, frozen in time against the plain stone wall of that chapel. Karsh said that he took it that way to capture the loneliness of the truly great artists and the loneliness of the exile.

Years later, when the portrait was on exhibition in the Museum of Fine Arts in Boston, another old, bald-headed man came day after day and stood for long moments at a time in front of the portrait. The curator of the museum noticed him and, when his curiosity got the best of him, went over, tapped the man on the shoulder, and asked why he stood so long before the picture. The old man, with obvious irritation, turned on the curator and said, "Hush, young man! Can't you see I'm listening to the music!"

Karsh watched Casals play his cello and presented a picture. The old man, looking at that picture, could hear the music.

The church ought to present a picture to the world of what God wants the world to be. And when we are that, we will provide the radical hope all humanity needs. Our music will then permeate the whole of life, and we will hasten the day when the kingdoms of this world will become the kingdom of our Lord and Christ, who will reign forever and ever.

97

8
Style: Some Distinctive Marks of a Wesleyan

For freedom Christ has set us free; stand fast therefore, and do not submit again to a yoke of slavery. Now I, Paul, say to you that if you receive circumcision, Christ will be of no advantage to you. I testify again to every man who receives circumcision that he is bound to keep the whole law. You are severed from Christ, you who would be justified by the law; you have fallen away from grace. For through the Spirit, by faith, we wait for the hope of righteousness. For in Christ Jesus neither circumcision nor uncircumcision is of any avail, but faith working through love. You were running well; who hindered you from obeying the truth? This persuasion is not from him who calls you. A little leaven leavens the whole lump (Gal. 5:1–9).

Circumstances sometimes call us to do strange things—things we would not otherwise do. Circumstances also cause us to do things we should have done but never got around to before.

Two out-of-town visitors were walking along a street in New York City late one night. One of the pair, wary of the reputation of city streets at night, kept glancing over his shoulder, nervously eyeing every alley and shadowed doorway. Sure enough, his anticipation was rewarded. As the two rounded the next corner, two muggers appeared out of the darkness and closed in. The nervous fellow knew what was going to happen. He reached for his wallet, pulled out a fifty-dollar bill, and handed it to his friend: "Joe, here's that fifty dollars I've been owing you for six months."

According to some critics, John Wesley never had an original idea in his life. He just borrowed from others. But the point is, whatever Wesley borrowed, he paid back tenfold and more. Even if it's true that Wesley only borrowed from others, that would hardly solve the riddle of this man and the spiritual dynamic of the Wesleyan movement. Wesley's genius and originality lay precisely in his borrowing, adapting, and combining diverse elements into a synthesis more dynamic than the sum of its parts.

Wesley also had the genius of putting an expansive, explosive truth in a single, sometimes simple sentence or a pithy phrase. He encapsulated his vision of mission and ministry in the sentence that has been on the lips of Wesleyans ever since: "The world is my parish." He borrowed from Paul to summarize his theology succinctly: "faith working through love." He gave a challenging and rather complete principle of stewardship in the crisp triplet: "Make all you can, save all you can, and give all you can."

He put controversy into perspective and defined what should be the position of every Christian in one terse line: "In essentials, unity; in nonessentials, liberty; in all things, charity." He described his whole approach to differences in belief and church order in the one question: "Is thine heart right, as my heart is with thy heart? . . . If it be, give me thine hand."[1]

In this chapter, we will look at the *style* of a Wesleyan. Style can be as important as content. There is a sense in which the "medium is the message."

Diana Vreeland, the undisputed leader in fashion, has written her autobiography with the simple but stylish title, *DV*. It records her lifetime of living with inimitable style. She emphasizes the importance of style by referring to Japan. "God was fair to the Japanese," she said. "He gave them no oil, no coal, no diamonds, no gold, no material resources—

nothing! Nothing comes from the island that you can sustain a civilization on. All God gave the Japanese was a sense of style."[2] It was the ultimate compliment to the Japanese from this fashion style-setter.

Wesleyans have a style that, to a marked degree, defines our uniqueness. As we look at some distinctive ingredients that make up that style, hold in your mind the fact that these marks are to be seen in the context of all the essential things we've been talking about in the preceding chapters.

A CATHOLIC SPIRIT

The first ingredient is a catholic spirit. This is a celebrated aspect of our style. This spirit is desperately needed in our day, because too many Christians are plagued with *xenophobia*.

You didn't know the church was plagued with xenophobia, did you? It's not a common word in our vocabulary. I thought about it recently when I saw a TV special on all the phobias that psychologists and psychiatrists are helping people deal with. A *phobia* is an exaggerated and persistent aversion to or dread and fear of something. Common ones that psychologists deal most frequently with are *acrophobia*, the fear of high places; *claustrophobia,* the fear of closed-in places; *dernophobia*, the fear of crowds; *autophobia*, the fear of self or of being alone; and *mysophobia*, the fear of contamination. Numerous others are the source of great emotional problems. I learned a new one recently—*gamophobia,* the fear of marriage.

But back to xenophobia. *Xenophobia* is a "hatred or distrust of foreigners or strangers." Practically speaking, it is a fear of that which is different from yourself, the fear and suspicion of differences. It has been the phobia of people from the beginning, and still is. Xenophobia has plagued the church.

Peter and the Jerusalem apostles feared Paul and his work among the Gentiles. They were suspicious because they did not understand. That spirit within the church has often hindered the ministry of Christ. We fear opinions, positions, attitudes, and beliefs that do not match our own.

Over against xenophobia I want to put those celebrated words of John Wesley. "Is thine heart right, as my heart is with thy heart? . . . If it be, give me thine hand." Those words are actually from 2 Kings 10:15. Wesley used them as the text for one of the noblest sermons he ever preached, his sermon "Catholic Spirit."[3]

I should make two points about the catholic spirit that is such an important part of the Wesleyan style:

First, one of the real confusions within Wesleyanism today is a misunderstanding and a misapplication of Wesley's concept of the catholic spirit. We mistakenly interpret that to mean theological pluralism, and we project such a pluralism to be both acceptable and desirable. Taken to an extreme, this concept has a fallacy. The way it is projected suggests that a Wesleyan Christian can believe almost anything about God, Jesus Christ, and the essential doctrines that relate to salvation. But this is a perversion of Wesley's idea of the catholic spirit.

Such an uncritical, undemanding, unexamined emphasis on so-called pluralism was the furthest thing from Wesley's thinking. He was unreserved in his condemnation of what he called "*speculative* latitudinarianism," which would be his word for the way many interpret pluralism today. Wesley said:

> A catholic spirit is not *speculative* latitudinarianism. It is not an indifference to all opinions: this is the spawn of hell, not the offspring of heaven. This unsettledness of thought, this being "driven to and fro and tossed about with every wind of doctrine" is a great curse, not a blessing; an irreconcilable enemy, not a friend, to true catholicism. A man of a truly catholic spirit has not now his religion to seek. He is fixed as the sun in his judgment concerning the main branches of Christian doctrine. It is true, he is always ready to hear and weigh whatsoever

can be offered against his principles; but as this does not show any wavering in his own mind, so neither does it occasion any. He does not halt between two opinions, nor vainly endeavor to blend them into one. Observe this, you who know not what spirit ye are of: who call yourselves men of the catholic spirit, only because you are of a muddy understanding; because your mind is all in a mist; because you have no settled, consistent principles, but are for jumbling all opinions together. Be convinced, that you have quite missed your way; you know not where you are. You think you are got into the very spirit of Christ when, in truth, you are nearer the spirit of Antichrist. Go, first, and learn the first elements of the gospel of Christ, and then shall you learn to be of a truly catholic spirit.[4]

My second point is this: Nothing is more needed in the church today, especially in the United States, than a catholic spirit. You will recall that in his pamphlet "The Character of a Methodist," Wesley said: "As to all opinions which do not strike at the root of Christianity, we think and let think." Remember now, Wesley was talking about things that do not strike at the root of Christianity.

102

- Does our mode of baptism—*how* we baptize—strike at the root of Christianity?

- Does whether or not we have musical instruments in the church make any difference as far as real Christianity is concerned?

- How we serve Communion—is that a grave issue as far as the faith is concerned?

- Is any argument about the Millennium essential to the Christian faith?

- Does it help to try to figure out when the Lord is going to come again? Is that kind of argument really a positive contribution to the kingdom?

Most of the things that we get all stirred up about, things that drive us to anger and even divide us as Christians—most of that, I think, the Lord cares little about. Remember what Jesus said to those Pharisees who condemned Him for plucking grain on the Sabbath so that His disciples might eat? "The sabbath was made for man, not man for the sabbath" (Mark 2:27). This is what Paul was saying in Galatians 5:1: "For freedom Christ has set us free; stand fast therefore, and do not submit again to a yoke of slavery." And how gloriously and powerfully did he write, "For in Christ Jesus neither circumcision nor uncircumcision is of any avail, but faith working through love" (v. 6).

This is what Wesley was getting at when he admonished his Methodist flock, "For opinions, or terms, let us not destroy the work of God. Dost thou love and serve God? It is enough. I give thee the right hand of fellowship."[5]

We need that spirit as Wesleyans. The world needs it— the catholic spirit lived out in our different denominations.

HEARTFELT RELIGION

The second ingredient of a Wesleyan style is what we often call "heartfelt religion." In Wesleyan language, this is the experience of the "warm heart." This has meaning at two points: the individual; and the fellowship, the larger group.

The Methodist movement was born in England and soon began to burn with a fire of love across the land, in large part, because of two big problems in the established church. One was *spiritual apathy*. Deism had flavored the intellectual and religious climate. God had become a benevolent ruler of the universe, removed from personal experience. In the arrogant rationalism that pervaded the day, everything had to be utterly reasonable.

The second thing that had happened was that *the church as an organization had become remote,* removed from life, not touching the people where they were. One cleric, for instance, had been made a bishop and given a lifetime stipend, but he never set foot in the diocese over which he presumably had spiritual and temporal oversight. It was obviously all temporal and nothing spiritual.

Into that setting with those two characteristics—spiritual apathy and a remote church structure—came the Wesleyan revival with an answer to these two glaring, devastating failures of the church.

For spiritual apathy, there was the experience of the warm heart. People wanted desperately not only to hear the gospel, but also to experience it. So Aldersgate became the model: "I felt my heart strangely warmed. I felt I did trust in Christ, Christ alone, for my salvation; and an assurance was given me that he had taken away *my* sins, even *mine,* and saved *me* from the law of sin and death." That experience was repeated over and over again.

Furthermore, for people who experienced a church that had become lifelessly formal at best, and coldly remote at worst, the Methodists came with ministries of care and warm concern. The class meetings and bands of the Methodist societies became the settings for these expressions of compassion. People cared for and looked after one another's souls. Loving hearts set other hearts on fire.

When Wesley spoke of "social holiness" and "social Christianity," he was pointing to New Testament *koinonia.* Christian fellowship meant not merely corporate worship, but watching over one another in love, advising, exhorting, admonishing, and praying with the brothers and sisters. "This, and this alone, is Christian fellowship," he said. And this is what Wesleyanism promoted. "We introduced Christian fellowship where it was utterly destroyed," said Wesley. And the fruits of it have been peace, joy, love, and zeal for good word and work.[6]

We need to ask, Is this style of the warm heart pronounced enough in our congregations and in ourselves? And a second question: Are we providing the structures of care where persons can grow in grace and discipleship, where the fruits of the Spirit can be cultivated?

These are the questions Paul addressed: "For in Christ Jesus neither circumcision nor uncircumcision is of any avail, but faith working through love. You were running well; who hindered you from obeying the truth?" (Gal. 5:6–7).

In a lecture at Emory University, Dr. Theodore Runyon introduced what to me was a whole new way of thinking about the "heart strangely warmed" and structures of care as means for our growth in Christ and our life in the world. It is a new way of thinking about a Wesleyan style. He used three terms to make an important distinction: *orthodoxy, orthopraxis,* and *orthopathy*. The first two terms were familiar, but not the third. Orthodoxy is right doctrine, right opinion, right belief. But Wesleyans have never believed that orthodoxy was enough. God demands right action, right practice, right behavior—that is *orthopraxis*.

Wesley recognized that many who can only inadequately formulate their faith, nevertheless, live transformed lives in constant fellowship with God:

> I believe the merciful God regards the lives and tempers of men more than their ideas. I believe he respects the goodness of heart, rather than the clearness of head; and that if the heart of a man be filled (by the grace of God, and the power of his Spirit) with the humble, gentle, patient love of God and man, God will not cast him into everlasting fire . . . because his ideas are not clear, or because his conceptions are confused.[7]

Wesley concluded,

> I admit that "without holiness no man shall see the Lord." But I dare not add, "or without clear ideas."

This seems to place Wesley solidly on the side of orthopraxis and against dead orthodoxy.

In another sermon, he listed all the arguments given against aid to the poor, including the argument that most of the poor are not Christians but obstinate sinners. Wesley's rejoinder was, "Whether [the poor] will be finally lost or

105

saved, you are expressly commanded to feed the hungry and clothe the naked. If you can, and do not, whatever becomes of them, you shall go away into everlasting fire."[8]

Even with that kind of plea for orthopraxis, working faith, he always insisted that as faith without works is dead, works without faith profits nothing; that "all morality, all justice, mercy and truth—without faith—is of no value in the sight of God."

Neither orthodoxy nor orthopraxis alone is sufficient. And Runyon added that even together, they are not enough. There must be *orthopathy*. This means right passions, senses, tempers, dispositions and, in the larger sense, right experience. This, said Runyon, is the challenge to a theology of conversion:

> To recognize the crying need of humankind to be encountered and transformed by Christian faith in all aspects of their being, including the emotions, feelings, and experiences. Nothing less is a sign of the kingdom and its power in the midst of the present age. And nothing less than this kind of theology and experience ought to undergird our preaching, our Christian education, our evangelism and mission, and our witness and action for peace and justice.[9]

Runyon then gave three hallmarks for such an orthopathic theology. First, Wesley's "bookends" of *creation* and *kingdom,* the fundamental conviction that all creation is to be redeemed by Christ. The world and everything in it is to be brought under the lordship of Christ—not destroyed, but redeemed.

The second hallmark of orthopathy is realism about the present order of things. "We are a part of a world that has corrupted God's good creation and become insensitive and deaf to God's will and way."[10] The gospel forces us to see the alienation and estrangement of the present order and present the gospel necessity of being reborn into a new order.

Thus, the final hallmark of orthopathic theology is the

familiar word of John 3:7: "You must be born anew," or as The Amplified Bible has it, "You must all be born from above."

Runyon's insight helps us think clearly about how we provide the opportunities for the "heart strangely warmed" and the structures of care that will be settings for the transformation of our whole life and total experience. When Wesley insisted that "true Christianity cannot exist without the inward experience and the outward practice of justice, mercy, and truth," he brought orthodoxy, orthopraxis, and orthopathy together and gave us our marching orders.

OUR WORLDWIDE PARISH

There are many marks of Wesleyan style. In the next chapter, we will deal with discipline and means of grace, which are a part of our style. For now, let's look at one other distinctive mark. It is gathered up in Wesley's popular saying, "The world is my parish." That statement captures the style of the Wesleyan movement—a concern for all humankind, a spending of ourselves and our resources that all the world might be brought to Christ.

107

We need to know that Wesley came to this position "kicking and screaming." His decision to join Whitefield in preaching in the fields to the poor and to coal miners was a difficult one. He fought against it. Whitefield was having great success in reaching for Christ persons who had been ignored by the established church. He sent for John Wesley, knowing his preaching power and organizing skill. Up to that point, Wesley had preached only in regular church services while in England. Should he accept Whitefield's appeal and help with the open air meetings in Bristol? Charles insisted that he not do it. But John practiced what he preached. He called on the Christian fellowship for guidance. He submitted the decision to the Fetter Lane Society, and they decided he should go. Wesley's *Journal* for Saturday, March 31, reads:

In the evening, I reached Bristol, and met Mr. Whitefield there. I could scarce reconcile myself at first to this strange way of preaching in the fields, of which he set me an example on Sunday; having been all my life (until very lately) so tenacious of every point relating to decency and order, that I should have thought the saving of souls almost a sin if it had not been done in a church.[11]

Wesley spoke to a little society on Sunday evening using the Sermon on the Mount—"one pretty remarkable precedent of field-preaching," he observed, "though I suppose there were churches at that time also." The next day, Monday, Wesley reported in his *Journal*:

At four in the afternoon I submitted to be more vile, and proclaimed in the highways the glad tidings of salvation, speaking from a little eminence in a ground adjoining the city, to about three thousand people. The Scripture on which I spoke was this, . . . "The Spirit of the Lord is upon Me, because He hath anointed Me to preach the gospel to the poor."[12]

Snyder sums up what happened:

Characteristically, Wesley immediately began to organize. He formed a number of societies and bands and on May 9 acquired a piece of property where he built his "New Room" as a central meeting place. When Whitefield returned to America in August, Wesley was left totally in charge of the growing work. He divided his time between Bristol and London, concentrating on open-air preaching, organizing bands and speaking at night to an increasing number of societies.

The Wesleyan Revival had begun. From the beginning it was a movement largely for and among the poor, those whom "gentlemen" and "ladies" looked on simply as part of the machinery of the new industrial system. The Wesleys preached, the crowds responded and Methodism as a mass movement was born.[13]

That's what Wesleyanism is all about. It's a missional and evangelical witness that sees the world as our parish and every person in the world—rich and poor, educated and uneducated, without regard to race—as a person for whom Christ died.

My friend George Hunter has told this thrilling story, one of those lively vignettes of Wesleyan history that gives us our vision for now and the future:

> A great Methodist leader named C. C. McCabe was the leader of new church extension for the Methodist Episcopal Church in about 1881. . . . One particular day he was traveling to help launch a round of new church plantings in Oregon, Idaho, and Washington, when he picked up a newspaper that had recorded the speech delivered in Chicago by Robert G. Ingersoll, a famous philosopher and agnostic. . . . In this speech, Ingersoll contended that the churches of the United States of America were in a terminal condition and in another generation there would be few, if any, of them left, which, on the whole, would be a good thing. That incensed McCabe. He got off the train at the next town, went to the Western Union office, dictated a telegram, and sent it to Ingersoll. . . . The telegram read, "Dear Bob: In the Methodist Church we are starting more than one new congregation a day, and we propose to make it two. Signed, C. C. McCabe.—P. S. All hail the power of Jesus' name."

That was the first of many spirited exchanges and debates between them. The word about that telegram got out and there evolved a folk hymn, part of which went like this:

> *The infidels, a motley band,*
>   *In counsel met and said,*
> *The churches are dying across the land,*
>   *And soon, they'll all be dead.*
>
> *When suddenly a message came,*
>   *And caught them with dismay,*

Reading, "All hail the power of Jesus' name,
We're building two a day."

Chorus

We're building two a day, dear Bob,
We're building two a day.
All hail the power of Jesus' name,
We're building two a day.[14]

It has happened before. It can happen again. It *should* happen. It will happen again when we Wesleyans recover the warm heart, when we provide structures of love and care, and when we get a passion for ministry and mission, believing "the world is our parish."

9
Discipline and Means of Grace

Therefore, since we are surrounded by so great a cloud of witnesses, let us also lay aside every weight, and sin which clings so closely, and let us run with perseverance the race that is set before us, looking to Jesus the pioneer and perfecter of our faith, who for the joy that was set before him endured the cross, despising the shame, and is seated at the right hand of the throne of God.

Consider him who endured from sinners such hostility against himself, so that you may not grow weary or fainthearted. In your struggle against sin you have not yet resisted to the point of shedding your blood. And have you forgotten the exhortation which addresses you as sons?—

"My son, do not regard lightly the discipline of the Lord, nor lose courage when you are punished by him. For the Lord disciplines him whom he loves, and chastises every son whom he receives."

It is for discipline that you have to endure. God is treating you as sons; for what son is there whom his father does not discipline? If you are left without discipline, in which all have participated, then you are illegitimate children and not sons. Besides this, we have had earthly fathers to discipline us and we respected them. Shall we not much more be subject to the Father of spirits and live? For they disciplined us for a short time at their pleasure, but he disciplines us for our good, that we may share his holiness. For the moment all discipline seems painful rather than pleasant; later it yields the peaceful fruit of righteousness to those who have been trained by it.

Therefore lift your drooping hands and strengthen your weak knees, and make straight paths for your feet, so that what is lame may not be put out of joint but rather be healed. Strive for peace with all men, and for the holiness without which no one will see the Lord. See to it that no one fail to obtain the grace of God; that no "root of bitterness" spring up and cause trouble, and by it the many become defiled; that no one be immoral or irreligious like Esau, who sold his birthright for a single meal. For you know that afterward, when he desired to inherit the blessing, he was rejected, for he found no chance to repent, though he sought it with tears (Heb. 12:1–17).

As Wesleyans, we have an equal and zealous emphasis on personal and social holiness. Wesley said, "As tenacious of inward holiness as a mystic, of outward holiness as a Pharisee." Neither the mystic nor the Pharisee was a model championed by Wesley. Yet at times he came near the edge of mysticism, and certainly a good part of his life would reflect the model of a Pharisee who knew the law impeccably and sought diligently to keep it.

To put the two together in this fashion, I believe, is one of those flashes of genius that come out now and then in Wesley's writings. "As tenacious of inward holiness as a mystic, of outward holiness as a Pharisee." That's a picture we can live with and build upon. It is a picture to hold in our minds as we think about the place of discipline in the Christian life, and of means of grace as channels of growth and power.

In her usual disarmingly honest and challenging way, Mother Theresa painted the picture clearly in her confession: "Pray for me that I not loosen my grip on the hands of Jesus even under the guise of ministering to the poor."

112

Doesn't that say it? Isn't that our primary calling as Christians? Isn't that the only way we will get on in being the disciples Jesus calls us to be—gripping the hands of Jesus with such firmness that we can't help following His lead?

Following Him in that fashion requires discipline. Also, Christ and the church provide means of grace that assist us in the process, and that's our focus in this chapter: discipline and means of grace.

DISCIPLINE IS ESSENTIAL

First, let's put it all in the context of Scripture. Hebrews 12:1–2 is one of those majestic, moving passages to which we should return often to reflect upon, pray over, and immerse ourselves in. It is an almost perfect summary of the Christian life. Let it sing in your soul:

> Therefore, since we are surrounded by so great a cloud of witnesses, let us also lay aside every weight, and sin which clings so closely, and let us run with perseverance the race that is set before us, looking to Jesus the pioneer and perfecter of our faith, who for the joy that was set before him endured the cross, despising the shame, and is seated at the right hand of the throne of God (Heb. 12:1–2).

113

This passage is packed with meaning, and there is one clear call in it—a call for discipline. "Let us also lay aside every weight, and sin which clings so closely." That's discipline! "Let us run with perseverance the race that is set before us." That's discipline! "Looking to Jesus, the pioneer and perfecter of our faith." That's discipline! Be certain, then, of this: Discipline is not an option for the Christian; it is absolutely essential.

Lodge two truths in your mind: God uses; we choose. God uses events and circumstances to discipline us. We choose to discipline ourselves by using all the means of grace available.

First, God uses. There is a discipline for the Christian that God exercises. This is the crux of what the writer to the Hebrews was talking about when he quoted Proverbs 3:11–12: "My son, do not regard lightly the discipline of the Lord, nor lose courage when you are punished by him. For the Lord disciplines him whom he loves, and chastises every son whom he receives" (Heb. 12:5–6).

There is a mystery to all of this suffering, hardship, pain, defeat, failure, and other adversities that come unsparingly and appear to be poured out on some people far more than others. There is a mystery that we despair at seeking to probe. We respond in all sorts of ways: grim resignation, self-pity, a cynical stiff upper lip, cowering, a pitiful martyr complex. We often see personal misfortune, adversity, pain, and suffering as punishment from God for our sins—God's vindictive response to our failure or outright disobedience.

The common question is: Why is God punishing me? That's the wrong question. God may not be punishing me at all. The right question is: What is God trying to teach me in all this?

We can never solve the mystery of human suffering and the connection between suffering and God's disciplining us. We can waste all our energy and end up miserable cynics or pitiful martyrs by dwelling on the *why*. The Scripture from Hebrews points the way. Even if we resist the idea that all that comes to us comes to us from God (which I do resist), we can be assured that a loving God can use all that comes to us and can help us use it for our good. God "disciplines us for our good, that we may share his holiness. For the moment all discipline seems painful rather than pleasant; later it yields the peaceful fruit of righteousness to those who have been trained by it" (vv. 10–11). So, God uses events and circumstances to discipline us, but what we are primarily concerned about here is the call to the Christian to a deliberately disciplined life.

We have to deliberately choose to discipline ourselves. That was one of Wesley's primary concerns, and it was a distinctive emphasis of the early Wesleyan movement. It is one of the marks of a Wesleyan style—*deliberately chosen discipline*.

Wesley preached an interesting sermon in 1778 entitled "Some Account of the Late Work of God in North America." In it, he sought to relate the various dispensations of divine providence in the American colonies as far back as 1736. In the sermon, Wesley commented on the preaching of George Whitefield, which was one of the major contributing factors to the First Great Awakening in America. On Whitefield's last journey to America, the evangelist lamented that many had drawn back into perdition. Taking note of that, Wesley sought to account for this "falling away." This was his telling statement:

> And what wonder? For it was a true saying, which was common in the ancient church, "The soul and the body make a man; and the spirit and discipline make him a Christian." But those who were more or less affected by Mr. Whitefield's preaching had no discipline at all. They had no shadow of discipline; nothing of the kind. They were formed into no societies. They had no Christian connection with each other, nor were they ever taught to watch over each other's souls. So that if they fell into lukewarmness, or even into sin, he had none to lift him up. He might fall lower and lower, yea into hell, if he would; for who regarded it?[1]

There are few more insightful quotations of Wesley than this. It clearly shows his feeling about the necessity for discipline in the Christian life.

Wesley put a great emphasis on proclaiming the gospel, as did Whitefield. He never diminished preaching and teaching the Word. But he insisted upon the discipline of gathering with a class or a band. As the Wesleyan movement became more established, Wesley noted the deterioration of this discipline, and he warned against it:

> Never omit meeting your Class or Band; never absent yourself from any public meeting. These are the very sinews of our Society; and whatever weakens or tends to

weaken our regard for these, or our exactness in attending them, strikes at the very root of our community. . . . The private weekly meeting for prayer, examination, and particular exhortation has been the greatest means of keeping and confirming every blessing that was received by the word preached and diffusing it to others. . . . Without this religious connection and intercourse the most ardent attempts, by mere preaching, have proved no lasting use.[2]

Some warnings should be sounded. We must guard against turning our disciplines into an end. To be disciplined is not the goal; the goal is to stay close to Christ, to keep our lives centered in Him. We must guard against falling into a salvation-by-works pattern. Grace and faith are still the key. We are not saved by disciplines; we are saved by grace through faith.

THE MEANS OF GRACE

This leads to our next concern: the means of grace. Again, *God uses, we choose.* If we are to mature into wholeness, "to the measure of the stature of the fulness of Christ" (Eph. 4:13), if we are going to "put on the whole armor of God" (Eph. 6:11), we must avail ourselves of the "means of grace" that Christ and His church provide.

"Means of grace" is a phrase commonly used by Christians to describe the channels through which God's grace is conveyed to us. By "means of grace," Wesley meant "outward signs, words, or actions, ordained of God, and appointed for this end, to be the ordinary channels whereby He might convey to men, preventing, justifying, or sanctifying grace."[3]

Wesley never limited God's grace to these means, nor should we. God may use myriad ways of bestowing grace upon us. Yet, there are some specific ways that God enables us to grow in grace. In his sermon "The Means of Grace," Wesley insisted that the means of grace had no power within themselves. They were *means,* and using them did not guarantee growth. Use of them was not to be legalistic and/or mechanical, but as an opening of ourselves to God's activity in our lives. Wesley divided these ordinary means of grace into two categories: (1) *instituted* means of grace, or works of piety; and (2) *prudential* means of grace, or works of mercy.

WORKS OF PIETY

Let's look briefly at the five works of piety, the instituted means of grace, described in Wesley's sermon. First is *prayer.* Wesley said,

> All who desire the grace of God are to wait for it in the way of prayer. This is the express direction of our Lord. In the Sermon on the Mount, . . . [Jesus] adds, "Ask, and it shall be given you; seek, and ye shall find; knock, and it shall be opened unto you: for everyone that asketh receiveth; and he that seeketh findeth; and to him that knocketh, it shall be opened" (Matt. 7:7–8).[4]

Second is *Scripture.* We've said that Wesley was a man of "one Book." He wanted Wesleyans to be Bible people. In fact, early Wesleyans were referred to derisively as "Bible-moths."

Wesley's emphasis upon the primacy of Scripture was based on the conviction that through the Bible, God gives, confirms, and increases true wisdom. According to Paul's word to Timothy, the Scripture is "able to instruct you for salvation through faith in Christ Jesus" (2 Tim. 3:15).

Third is *the Lord's Supper.* Wesley said, "All who desire an increase of the grace of God are to wait for it in partaking of the Lord's Supper; for this also is a direction [Jesus] Himself hath given: . . . 'Do this in remembrance of me.' "[5] Paul put it this way: "For as often as you eat this bread and drink the cup, you proclaim the Lord's death until he comes" (1 Cor. 11:26).

Wesley believed that the Lord's Supper is a *confirming* experience and also a *converting* one. His mother, Susanna, received the gift of assurance at the Lord's Table. He said that

117

The Lord's Supper was ordained by God to be a means of conveying to persons either preventing, justifying, or sanctifying grace, according to their particular needs. The persons for whom it was ordained are all who know and feel that they need the grace of God. No fitness is required but a sense of our state of sinfulness and helplessness.[6]

The fourth instituted means of grace is *fasting*. This is the one most of us know least about from direct experience. "Of all the means of grace," Wesley said, "there is scarcely any concerning which persons have run into greater extremes than that of religious fasting." He continued:

> How have some exalted this beyond all Scripture and reason;—and others utterly disregarded it. . . . The truth lies between them both. . . . It is not the end, but it is a precious means thereto; a means which God has ordained, and in which, . . . when duly used, he will surely give us his blessing. . . .
>
> Let every season, either of public or private fasting, be a season of exercising all those holy affections which are implied in a broken and contrite heart. Let it be a season of devout mourning, of godly sorrow for sin; . . .
>
> And with fasting let us always join fervent prayer, pouring out our whole souls before God, confessing our sins with all their aggravations, humbling ourselves under his mighty hand, laying open before him all our wants, all our guiltiness and helplessness. This is a season for enlarging our prayers, both in behalf of ourselves and of our brethren.[7]

118

The final instituted means of grace is the *Christian conference*. This is small-group sharing in which the true *koinonia*, Christian fellowship, can take place. We referred to it when we talked about the church as the dwelling place of the wonder of Christian fellowship. The class meetings and bands of early Wesleyanism were the setting for this.

The importance Wesley placed in this means of grace can be seen in two remarks he made. On occasion, he stated that "preaching like an apostle without joining together those that are awakened and training them up in the ways of God, is only begetting children for the murderer." This was his opinion after a visit to Pembrokeshire where there were no regular societies. His evaluation was that "the consequence is that nine of the ten once-awakened are now faster asleep than ever." He was fully convinced that wherever this dimension of discipleship was lost, Methodism would cease to be a vital movement.[8]

Those are the works of piety, or the instituted means of grace: prayer, Scripture, the Lord's Supper, fasting, and Christian conferencing. Wesley gave instructions as to how these means should be used:

> First, always retain a lively sense, that God is above all means. Have a care, therefore, of limiting the Almighty. He does whatsoever and whensoever it pleaseth Him. . . .
>
> Secondly. Before you use any means, let it be deeply impressed on your soul,—there is no *power* in this. It is, in itself, a poor, dead, empty thing: separate from God, it is a dry leaf, a shadow. . . . But, because God bids, therefore I do; . . . I wait for His free mercy, whereof cometh my salvation. . . .
>
> Thirdly. In using all means, seek God alone. In and through every outward thing, look singly to the *power* of His Spirit, and the *merits* of His Son.[9]

WORKS OF MERCY

Now a word about the prudential means of grace, or works of mercy. Apart from attending upon all the ordinances of God, Wesley listed two: (1) doing no harm, and (2) doing good. Isn't that simple? Yet, how profound in implication!

It was clearly underscored in Hebrews. "Strive for peace with all men, and for the holiness without which no one will see the Lord. See to it that no one fail to obtain the grace of God; that 'no root of bitterness' spring up and cause trouble, and by it the many become defiled" (Heb. 12:14–15).

Put simply, the truth is this: *Acting as a Christian is a means of grace.* Have you ever thought of it that way? Our Christian faith expresses itself in what we do and in what we refuse to do. It is true, as the song says, "They will know we are Christians by our love." It is also true that what we refrain from doing may be the needed telling witness of our lives.

Often when Christians think about what they should *refrain* from doing, sins of the flesh come to mind. Refraining from those goes without saying. So let's look at some other areas:

- Refusing to order your social life around the cocktail circuit.

- Refraining from sharing, even in listening to, destructive gossip.

- Refusing to affirm the racial bigotry of those around us.

- Refusing to treat any person, whether a mate or an employee, as a thing rather than a person.

All of these may be means of conveying God's grace to our lives. I could go on. Suffice it to say that, in our everyday lives of acting as Christians, what we do and what we refrain from doing are means of grace. So there is a sense in which we act our way into Christlikeness. I've never known persons who studied their way into Christlikeness, or people who prayed or worshiped their way into Christlikeness. But I've known countless people who have *acted* their way into Christlikeness. The likeness of Christ shines forth from their lives. All of these people pray; some of them are people with a deep prayer life. They study to varying degrees. They worship. But most of all, they are people whose acts of mercy make them "look like" Jesus.

What we do or refuse to do in obedience to God becomes a channel of God's grace, which transforms us into the likeness of Christ. And likewise, what we do or refrain from doing in obedience to God becomes a channel for the grace of God to others.

Let me tell you about some of this grace being manifested at least indirectly through the congregation I serve in Memphis, Tennessee. The work of the United Methodist Neighborhood Center is a source of hope and life for countless people. What *grace* this work conveys! Our church is now supporting two full-time missionaries to the city, apart from our ongoing support of the center's work. Our newest staff person is Reverend Billy Joe Jackson. He has been there only a month, at the time of this writing. What a person of God he is! What commitment and what sanctified imagination! He is so excited, and his excitement is contagious. I thrilled as he talked recently about evangelism among the poor black people in the heart of our city.

Billy Joe has said his ministry is primarily twofold—a ministry of *miracles* and a ministry of *mercy*. He didn't know about Wesley's "works of mercy" category as a means of grace, but he was practicing it. He has started a study-prayer group with about twenty men, and they are praying for miracles—jobs for those who are unemployed, health for those who are sick, salvation for those who don't yet trust Christ.

And what about works of mercy? He is visiting people in their homes, entering into their lives and sharing God's Word and love. He is also standing with them in their time of need. The day before I last talked with him, he went to court with a man. His very presence seemed to cause the public defender assigned to this fellow to become more interested and more responsible. A man was given hope, and one act of mercy on the part of one person caused another to be gracious and caring.

The director of neighborhood centers, Mark Matheny, told me of an event that took place at the Bread of Life weekly luncheon (a weekly food program at the center in which members of our congregation participate) around Christmastime. A twenty-eight-year-old man was in dire need. He had been unemployed for months and couldn't find a job. One of our Sunday school classes had provided a special offering for

121

him as an act of mercy. But the same week a little girl had been stabbed to death in that community. The unemployed man, though his need was desperate, refused his gift and directed it to be given to the mother of the stabbed girl. *Mercy begets mercy.*

A sign in Latin over the doorway of a dining room in San Francisco says, "*Caritate Dei.*" This dining room is in St. Anthony's Catholic Church and feeds about one thousand needy folks each day. I read about a young mechanic from Chicago who went to San Francisco for a vacation, got drunk, was rolled, and ended up in jail without a penny. In jail, he learned of St. Anthony's and went there for a meal when he got out, before he headed back to Chicago. A woman began cleaning the adjoining table. "When do we get down on our knees, lady?" the Chicago mechanic called to her.

"You don't here."

He winked, pulled his red beard. "Then, when's the sermon, the lecture, huh?"

"Aren't any," she replied.

"What's the gimmick?" he persisted. His smile was hesitant; he looked uncomfortable.

The well-dressed woman brushed her hair back. She pointed to the Latin inscription over the entrance: *Caritate Dei.* The brash young traveler squinted up at it and slurred the unfamiliar words. "What's it mean, lady?"

"Out of love for God," she said with a smile, and moved to clear another table.

That's one way grace comes to us, and the way it comes to others, *in acts of mercy*; and that grace will eventually prevail. That's the style of Wesleyans—disciplined and using all the means of grace so that we might hold on to the hands of Christ and serve others "out of love for God."

Notes

Chapter 1

1. John Wesley, *Wesley's Fifty-Three Sermons,* ed. by Edward H. Sugden (Nashville: Abingdon, 1983). This quotation is taken from the preface to the sermons.

2. Ibid., p. 1.

3. *Book of Hymns,* no. 527.

4. D. Stuart Briscoe, "Romans," *The Communicator's Commentary,* vol. 6 (Waco: Word Books, 1981), pp. 93–94.

5. Ibid.

Chapter 2

1. *Time,* January 9, 1984, pp. 28–29.

2. "I Sought the Lord," *Book of Hymns,* no. 96, vv. 1–2.

3. William R. Cannon, *The Theology of John Wesley* (Lanham, Maryland: University Press of America, 1984), p. 93.

4. William Barclay, *The Epistle to the Romans,* vol. 7 of *The Daily Study Bible* (Philadelphia: Westminster Press, 1955), p. 54.

5. *Wesley's Fifty-Three Sermons,* p. 23.

Chapter 3

1. *Wesley's Fifty-Three Sermons,* p. 558.

2. W. E. H. Lecky, *A History of England in the 18th Century* (London: Longmans, Green and Company, 1892), 3:122.

3. Albert C. Outler, *Theology in the Wesleyan Spirit* (Nashville: Discipleship Resources, 1975), p. 37.

4. John Calvin, *Institutes of the Christian Religion,* vol. 2 (Grand Rapids: Eerdmans, 1953), p. 3.

5. John Wesley, *Notes on the New Testament* (Grand Rapids: Baker, 1983), p. 489.

6. Sermon 128, sec. 24.

7. Cannon, *Theology of Wesley*, p. 95.

8. Sermon 118, sec. 25.

9. *Wesley's Fifty-Three Sermons*, p. 566.

10. "And Can It Be That I Should Gain," *Book of Hymns*, no. 527, v. 1.

Chapter 4

1. "Original Sin," *Wesley's Fifty-Three Sermons*, p. 565.

2. Outler, *Theology in the Wesleyan Spirit*, p. 57.

3. *Wesley's Fifty-Three Sermons*, p. 510.

4. Ibid., p. 511.

5. Ibid.

6. Ibid., p. 512.

7. Ibid.

8. "The New Birth," *Wesley's Fifty-Three Sermons*, p. 567.

9. Ibid., p. 573.

10. Outler, *Theology in the Wesleyan Spirit*, p. 58.

11. Ibid.

12. John Wesley, "The New Birth," *Wesley's Standard Sermons,* ed. by Edward H. Sugden, in *The Works of Wesley,* 18 vols. (Grand Rapids: Zondervan, 1986–   ), 2:240.

13. Steve Harper, *John Wesley's Message for Today* (Grand Rapids: Zondervan, 1983), pp. 95–96.

14. "Love Divine, All Loves Excelling," *Book of Hymns*, no. 283, v. 4.

Chapter 5

1. Loren Eiseley, *The Immense Journey* (New York: Random House, 1957), pp. 174–5.

2. "On Sin in Believers," *Wesley's Standard Sermons*, 2:369.

3. *Wesley's Fifty-Three Sermons*, p. 665.

4. Ibid., pp. 671–2.

5. Ibid., p. 216.

6. *Book of Hymns*, no. 224, v. 1.

7. Robert Southey, *Life of Wesley*, 2 vols. (New York: Harper and Brothers, 1847), 2:180f.

8. Nehemiah Curnock, ed., *The Journal of John Wesley*, 8 vols. (London: Epworth Press, 1909–16), 1:476–7.

9. "Jesus, Lover of My Soul," *Book of Hymns*, no. 125, v. 1.

10. Robert G. Tuttle, Jr., *John Wesley: His Life and Theology* (Grand Rapids: Zondervan, 1978), p. 200.

11. Thomas Jackson, ed., *The Works of John Wesley*, 14 vols. (Grand Rapids: Baker, n.d.), 1:104.

12. "Where Shall My Wondering Soul Begin," *Book of Hymns*, no. 528, v. 1.

Chapter 6

1. John Telford, ed., *The Letters of John Wesley*, 8 vols. (London: Epworth Press, 1931), 2:325.

2. Quoted by Thomas A. Langford, ed., *Wesleyan Theology: A Sourcebook* (Durham, North Carolina: Labyrinth Press, 1984), p. 13.

3. Jackson, ed., *The Works of John Wesley*, 8:31.

4. Colin W. Williams, *John Wesley's Theology Today* (Nashville: Abingdon, 1960), p. 151.

5. Albert C. Outler, *John Wesley* (New York: Oxford University, 1964), pp. 180–81.

6. Jim Wallace, *Called to Conversion* (New York: Harper and Row, 1981).

7. William Sloan Coffin, quoted by Don Shelby in his sermon, "Lord, You Can't Mean Hate," February 18, 1979.

Chapter 7

1. Roy H. Short, *History of the Council of Bishops* (Nashville: Abingdon, 1980), pp. 62–63.

2. Jackson, ed., *The Works of Wesley*, 7:205.

THE CHRISTIAN WAY

3. Howard A. Snyder, *The Radical Wesley* (Downers Grove, Illinois: InterVarsity, 1980), p. 143.

4. Ibid., p. 144.

5. Quoted by Charles Colson in *Loving God* (Grand Rapids: Zondervan, 1984), p. 123.

6. Dag Hammarskjöld, *Markings* (New York: Knopf, 1964), p. 122.

7. Quoted by Albert C. Outler, "Wilson Lectures," p. 16.

8. Jackson, ed., *The Works of John Wesley,* 9:325.

9. Ibid., 5:296.

10. Quoted by Lovett Weems in *The Gospel According to Wesley.*

11. Quoted by S. Paul Schilling in *Methodism and Society in Theological Perspective* (Nashville: Abingdon, 1960), p. 64.

12. Jackson, ed., *The Works of John Wesley,* 13:153.

13. William H. Willimon, "In But Not of the World," *Circuit Rider* (November-December 1982), 8–9.

14. "One Holy Church of God Appears," *Book of Hymns,* no. 296, v. 4.

Chapter 8

1. John Wesley, "The Character of a Methodist," quoted by Langford, *Wesleyan Theology,* p. 19.

2. Excerpt from *DV,* by Dana Vreeland, *House and Garden* (April 1984), 36.

3. It was one of the few instances in Wesley's preaching when the scriptural setting of the text had nothing to do with the sermon. Unlike most of us preachers, Wesley usually didn't take a text and depart from it; he stayed with it. But that was not so in this instance. Wesley took the words completely out of their grisly context in 2 Kings 10 and asked, not what they meant there, but what a follower of Christ should find in them today. And from that exploration, he gave us a great word to guide us as we think about the catholic spirit. "Catholic Spirit," Sugden, ed., *Wesley's Standard Sermons,* 2:142–3.

4. Sugden, ed., *Wesley's Standard Sermons,* 2:142–3.

5. Langford, *Wesleyan Theology,* p. 19.

126

6. Snyder, *The Radical Wesley*, p. 127.

7. Jackson, ed., *The Works of John Wesley*, 7:354.

8. Ibid., p. 307.

9. Unpublished lecture by Theodore H. Runyon, Jr., Candler School of Theology.

10. Ibid.

11. Quoted by Snyder, *The Radical Wesley*, p. 33.

12. Ibid.

13. Ibid.

14. George G. Hunter III, "The Challenge We Face," *The Advance* vol. 31, no. 4:9–10.

Chapter 9

1. Jackson, ed., *The Works of John Wesley*, 7:411.

2. Ibid., 11:433.

3. Sugden, ed., *Wesley's Standard Sermons*, 2:245.

4. Ibid., 1:242.

5. Ibid., 2:251.

6. Jackson, ed., *The Works of John Wesley*, 1:279–80.

7. Ibid., 5:345, 359, 360.

8. Harper, *John Wesley's Message for Today*, p. 84.

9. Sugden, ed., *Wesley's Standard Sermons*, 1:259, 260.